# practical GUIDE to MAKING money on the MOBILE internet

David Smith

**bango** press

Cambridge, UK

Practical Guide to Making Money on the Mobile Internet
by David Smith

Published by Bango Press, 5 Westbrook Centre, Cambridge CB4 1YG, UK.
Tel: +44 1223 472777   http://www.bango.com

## Legal Notices

Copyright © 2005 Bango.net Limited. All rights reserved. No part of this book may be reproduced or transmitted in any form or by any means, electronic, mechanical, including photocopying, recording, or by any information storage or retrieval system without prior written permission from the publisher.

The ● symbol, "Bango" and the Bango logo are trademarks or registered trademarks of Bango.net Limited.

David Smith asserts the moral right to be recognised as the author of this work.

## Notice of Liability

Every effort has been made to ensure that this book contains accurate and current information. However, Bango and the author shall not be liable for any loss or damage suffered by readers as a result of any information contained herein.

## British Library Cataloguing in Publication Data

A catalogue record for this book is available from the British Library.

## Printing history

| | |
|---|---|
| April 2004 | First edition |
| May 2004 | Second edition |
| September 2004 | Third edition |
| April 2005 | Fourth edition |

Printed and bound in the United Kingdom by Antony Rowe Ltd, Eastbourne
ISBN: 0-9547930-0-5

# Contents

**Foreword**     ix

# Introduction

**About this book**     3
    Mobile internet opportunity     4
    What's in this book     4
    Who should read this book?     4

**Success stories**     7
    The Sun     7
    Groove Gaming     8
    Maxim     9
    Get!Guide     10

**How is it done?**     11
    The "browse and buy" model     11
    How does Bango fit in?     12
    Using Bango to make money     13

# Creating your site

**Introducing WML**     17
    What is WML?     17
    Tagging basics     19
    A simple "Hello World!" WML file     21
    "Hello again, World!": adding links and images     25
    Timers and events     26
    Hints and tips     27
    Summary     28

**Structuring your mobile internet site**     29
    The home page     29
    Sections of your site     30
    New content     31
    Popular content     32
    Loss leaders: free content     32
    Thumbnails and teasers     33

## Building a free-content site — 35
Phone compatibility — 35
Testing your site — 36
"Free Hollywood"—a complete site — 37
Summary — 45

## Adding chargeable content using the Bango Service — 47
Bango packages — 47
Bango Numbers — 48
The Members' Lounge web site — 49
Buying a Bango package — 50
"Hollywood Reloaded" — 52
Typical user experience — 55
Checking revenue — 57
Limitations — 57
Creating a dynamic site — 58
Summary — 59

## Content ratings and access restrictions — 61
Introduction — 61
Bango services — 62
Mobile operator rules and regulations — 63
Rating guidelines — 63
Rating your content — 64

## The Bango Relay Service — 65
What is the Bango Relay Service? — 65
Benefits of the Bango Relay Service — 66
Bango Relay Service inputs and outputs — 67
Information passing with the p parameter — 68
Detecting your customers using the u parameter — 69
Increasing security using the t parameter — 70
Dynamic pricing with the c parameter — 70
Changing access limits using the na and ta parameters — 72
Page and content titles using the pt and ct parameters — 72
Assigning Bango Relay functionality to a Bango Number — 73
Improvements to the Bango Relay Service — 73

## The Bango Identifier Service — 75
Bango Identifier Service inputs and outputs — 75

| | |
|---|---:|
| Information passing with the p parameter | 76 |
| Manual login and the login parameter | 77 |
| Identifying your customers using the u parameter | 77 |
| Trusting identity using the t parameter | 77 |
| Checking barring status with the a parameter | 78 |
| Confirming identification with the id parameter | 78 |
| Assigning Bango Identifier functionality to a Bango Number | 79 |

## Security and digital rights management — 81

| | |
|---|---:|
| Digital rights management | 81 |
| Unauthorised access | 82 |
| Protecting your content | 83 |
| Summary | 86 |

# Attracting customers to your site—and keeping them

## The three Cs: customers, content, chutzpah — 89

| | |
|---|---:|
| Customers, customers, customers | 89 |
| Content, content, content | 93 |
| Chutzpah, chutzpah, chutzpah | 95 |

## Choosing a Bango Number you can promote — 97

| | |
|---|---:|
| Standard, Bronze, Silver and Gold numbers | 98 |
| Bango packages | 98 |
| Phone spelling: Bango Numbers are also words | 99 |
| Making use of your brand | 99 |
| What service do you provide? | 100 |
| What's your phone number? | 100 |
| T9 hassles | 100 |

## Simple promotion of your Bango Number — 103

| | |
|---|---:|
| The Bango symbol | 103 |
| Where to promote your Bango Number | 105 |
| The user experience | 105 |
| Effectiveness | 107 |

## The Bango Txt Trigger and Web Trigger services — 109

| | |
|---|---:|
| Overview | 109 |
| How to promote your site | 110 |
| User experience | 112 |

| | |
|---|---:|
| Contacting your customers | 113 |
| The Global Txt Trigger Service | 114 |
| The Bango Web Trigger Service | 115 |
| Effectiveness | 115 |

## Viral marketing — 117
| | |
|---|---:|
| What is viral marketing? | 117 |
| Viral marketing myths | 118 |
| The Tipping Point | 119 |
| Send to a friend | 120 |
| Examples | 121 |
| Effectiveness | 122 |

## The Bango Directory and World of Content — 123
| | |
|---|---:|
| What is the Bango Directory? | 123 |
| Adding your site to the Bango Directory | 124 |
| Selecting appropriate keywords | 125 |
| How search results are ranked | 126 |
| "Top 4" keyword auctions | 127 |
| User experience | 128 |

## Charging your customers — 131
| | |
|---|---:|
| What parts of the site should remain free? | 131 |
| What should I charge for? | 132 |
| Charging options | 133 |
| The Bango Txt Subscription Service | 134 |
| How much to charge? | 136 |
| Using the Members' Lounge to set charges | 136 |
| Currency issues | 138 |

## Tracking site usage — 139
| | |
|---|---:|
| What's available in the Members' Lounge? | 139 |
| Turning data into information | 140 |
| Categorising customers | 143 |

## Doing business with Bango — 145
| | |
|---|---:|
| Paying for Bango packages | 145 |
| Your earnings | 146 |
| Paying package fees using your earnings | 147 |
| VAT | 148 |

# Appendixes

## Device information — 153
The WURFL — 153
UAProf — 156
Which to use? — 157

## Web server issues — 159
Directory index files — 159
WML-related MIME types — 160

## Bango Txt Trigger guidelines and requirements — 163
ICSTIS code of practice — 163

## Payment for your content — 165
Premium reverse SMS — 165
Operator billing systems — 166
Debit/credit cards — 166
PIN codes — 167

# Foreword

The mobile internet provides one of the best opportunities ever for online entrepreneurs. Within a few years, almost everybody on the planet will be able to reach your service from the palm of their hand.

The cost of creating and running a mobile site is small—you can get going for about the cost of renting a market stall for a few days.

You can collect money very easily using the Bango Service which is described in this book. Users can pay from the price of a chocolate bar up to the price of a gourmet meal immediately on their phone. With colour, Java, good quality audio, videos and all sorts of new features on phones you can deliver a great service. You can market directly to your potential users, and they can communicate with you through your site or through text messages.

We are at the beginning of a gigantic, fast moving market with few barriers to entry. You have first mover advantage and can steal a march on the "big guys". By producing a great service or product, you can either earn lots of money and become a "global gorilla" or sell your company to those who are bigger but move later.

The only challenges that remain are your "big idea" and the three P's "Promote, Promote, Promote". I can't help you with the big idea, but with tools like the Bango Txt Trigger Service, the Bango Directory and above all the "Send to a friend" viral marketing support, you have a range of promotion options unparalleled in the history of the internet.

Good Luck!

Ray Anderson, *Founder and CEO of Bango*

PS—When you have made your millions, please don't forget to invite me to visit your yacht in the South of France!

Part I
# Introduction

# Chapter 1
# About this book

This book has one major goal: to help you make money from the mobile internet.

After a shaky start, the mobile internet is growing rapidly. Millions of people world-wide can now access web sites from their mobile phones. Phone technology is improving so fast that the negative stories of a few years ago—of feeling like you're looking at a web site through a keyhole—are fading from the memory. Today's phones have larger, colour screens and many more features than their predecessors. And web site owners are now much more willing to offer specially designed sites for mobile access.

More and more people are beginning to realise that there's money to be made on the mobile internet. Mobile shops are springing up everywhere—sites where you can browse and try before you buy, with easy payment and instant download. A great many of these sites use the services of Bango: Bango takes care of all the money matters, leaving them to grow their sites.

This book is about how you can join them: build your site, promote your site and make money using Bango's services.

In these pages you won't find a "get rich quick" scheme. We all know—and even the dot.com venture capitalists have learned—that nothing is certain except death, taxes and hyperbolic marketing. To make money you need ideas, effort and some luck.

We'll try to help you harness your ideas and apply your effort in the right places. You may still need some luck, but we'll try to remove as much uncertainty as we can.

# Mobile internet opportunity

The Mobile Data Association (http://www.mda-mobiledata.org) predicted that by the end of 2004 about 1.6 billion people—a quarter of the world's population—would have mobile phones. In the UK, mobile internet usage hit 46 million WAP page impressions per day in January 2005, a 60% increase on the previous January. According to Nokia, more people can now connect to the internet from their mobile phone than from a PC.

That means more people will be phoning, texting and surfing from mobile phones. And it means that more people will be searching for content to buy.

People expect everything for free on the fixed internet of PCs and Macs—it's a legacy of the origins of the system. But that's not true with mobile access. People expect to pay for phone calls, and they're happy to pay to download content to their phones. Ringtones, images, news, information, videos, games, chat, dating services—all available, all chargeable.

# What's in this book

This book has four parts:

- Part I includes some success stories for those who've made it on the mobile internet, and shows how they've done it.

- Part II shows how to build from scratch a mobile internet site that integrates with Bango's systems. We include demonstration sites that you can try out from your phone and use as a starting point for your own sites if you wish.

- Part III helps you learn how to attract customers to your site. It lists various ways you can promote your site, how you can spot trends and track revenue, and it also deals with business issues such as tax.

- Part IV contains appendixes of useful information.

# Who should read this book?

Anyone who wants to build or promote a money-making mobile internet site should read this book.

- Part I is suitable for everyone.

- Part II is aimed more at a technical audience: the site-builders writing the code.
- Part III is more suitable for a non-technical audience: those promoting the site.
- Part IV contains both technical and non-technical appendixes.

The book assumes the reader is familiar with internet usage—both the fixed internet accessed from PCs or Macs and the mobile internet accessed from mobile phones.

## Chapter 2
# Success stories

In this short chapter we'll introduce you to some mobile internet success stories and show how they make money.

## The Sun

*The Sun* newspaper, part of the News International group, has nine million readers each day and also has a strong presence on the fixed internet with its Sun Online site. From this position of strength, it saw potential for a mobile channel to produce an important new revenue stream for Sun-branded content—content that was designed specifically for mobile phone users.

Developed by Blue Star Mobile, Sun Mobile is a browse-and-buy mobile portal featuring ringtones, Java games, wallpapers and images of Page 3 babes. Bango provides fast, easy access to the site and handles content charging so users anywhere in the world can pay for Sun-branded content.

"It's vitally important that *The Sun* has a strong presence in all media—be it print, web or mobile," said Simon Ashley at News International. "The new browse and buy site gives us a direct, interactive relationship with our customers on mobile and allows us to develop the Sun brand's awareness within the youth market."

*The Sun* also wanted to capitalise on the cross-fertilization between the web and mobile channels. Over three million people a day access the Sun Online web site, with approximately 50% of these coming from the US and Canada. Bango's ability to provide easy access from these countries and collect payment from users, whatever network they choose, means that *The Sun* can drive extra revenue by promoting Sun Mobile to their web readers.

To access the Sun Mobile site, text "go sun" to short code 83055 in the UK or text "go sun" to +44 7786 203222 elsewhere in the world.

## Groove Gaming

LDC Games is a distributor of mobile games. Its product portfolio includes leading gaming titles from Gamesloft—such as *Tom Clancey's Splinter Cell* and *Prince of Persia*—and some excellent games from Korea, one of the major gaming centres in the world. The company saw an opportunity to grow the business based on mobile games because although mobile versions of leading titles were being produced, there was no aggressive strategy to develop the mobile marketplace. LDC wanted a consumer brand for their range of mobile games and decided upon Groove Gaming as the brand.

Groove Gaming wanted a fast way for people to pay and download the game on their phone and provide their target audience of 18-30 year olds with a totally mobile experience. Above all, they didn't want to spend time and resources integrating with various billing solutions as they had no expertise in this area.

The company also wanted to use a range of traditional media such as print advertising and radio promotions to generate interest in their products, and to drive people to their mobile site using text messages.

Bango provides Groove Gaming with a browse and buy mobile environment. People interested in buying a game featured in a promotion text "go groove" to 83055 on their mobile phone and receive a special message that takes them straight to the Groove Gaming WAP site. There they can browse the games, pay for the one they want and download it straight to their phone.

Groove Gaming tracks the revenue from each promotional campaign by having a different "call-to-action" for each. This allows the company to easily measure the most effective ways to promote their games.

## Maxim

Maxim is a world-wide hit with lads looking for their favourite pin-up girl. Dennis Publishing, well known as a forward-thinking publisher, publishes Maxim in the UK. Realising that mobile was the next big trend, it asked Mobile Media International to develop a mobile site that would give people access to a catalogue of over 500 wallpapers of Maxim Girls plus up-to-date news from Maxim magazine.

The Maxim mobile site is powered by Bango's browse and buy capability which provides the same shopping experience as an operator portal, with the advantage that users on any network, anywhere in the world, can access and pay for content.

Traffic to the Maxim mobile site is driven by promotions on the Maxim web site and in the magazine. Readers can either access a wallpaper of a particular Maxim Girl and from there browse to see what else is available, or they can go straight to the mobile site and browse around the portfolio of Maxim girls before choosing to buy and download wallpapers.

The successful "Little Black Book" promotion enabled readers to date a Maxim Girl in their local area. The Little Black Book was distributed with Maxim magazine in 2005 and readers who texted Maxim with the name of their favourite girl were pushed to a page on the mobile site where they viewed info on the girl plus an opportunity to date her.

The Maxim site recognises returning users, allowing Maxim to customise the site and optimise the service depending on the user's mobile network and phone type.

To access the Maxim Mobile site, text "go maxim" to short code 83055 in the UK or text "go maxim" to +44 7786 203222 elsewhere in the world.

# Get!Guide

Based in New York, USA, Get!Guide runs a directory to the mobile internet. Get!Guide sets out to make the whole process of traversing the mobile web extremely easy. It has developed intuitive software that not only figures out what you want but also makes it easy to get there using the fewest number of clicks on your mobile phone.

Get!Guide also keeps your favourite links on the front page for easy access. The more you click on a directory link, the higher it ranks on your mobile screen—so the items you click on most sit at the top of your screen and are easy to find. Get!Guide also allows you to remove any link or category that you might find offensive, and password-protect it, so the whole directory can be made child safe.

Get!Guide chose Bango to charge for access to its global service. Since Get!Guide launched, its sales have been growing exponentially. Bango-enabled content providers can visit the Get!Guide site at http://www.getguide.net and register their site to be listed in the Get!Guide directory. Users can text "go guide" to +44 7786 203222 or visit bango.net/guide on their phone.

# Chapter 3
# How is it done?

How can you follow in the footsteps of the success stories in Chapter 2, and build your own profitable business from the mobile internet?

Let's start with a simple observation. The marketplace has been at the central core of communities across the planet for all of recorded history. From a few stallholders on a village green to global trading of stocks and shares, markets are everywhere.

Leaving aside specialist marketplaces like the stock market and money trading, look at your own personal experience. When you visit a market—a town or village market, a supermarket, or a shopping mall—what do you do? Do you make a beeline for the one thing you came for? Unlikely. Like everyone else in the market, you browse. You may have a list of things to buy, but that doesn't stop you looking—and perhaps buying—more.

What successful markets understand is that a marketplace isn't just a place to buy and sell. It's a place to *browse*, buy and sell. Browsing helps you get an emotional *feel* for a place: and once you've hooked someone emotionally they'll return for more. (Notice how people talk about their *favourite* shops, or how they *love* or *hate* them—hardly an emotionless, logical viewpoint.)

## The "browse and buy" model

Recognising that you need a "browse and buy" model for your mobile content business is an important step towards building the emotional connections that bring a strong, loyal customer base.

The importance of the "browse and buy" model is shown by some recent research. Before this model, mobile content was sold through advertising and with one-off purchases, often over premium-rate phone lines. One of the leading ringtone providers, ringtones.co.uk, reported that only 18% of people went through this process more than once: in other words, in the old model, 8 in 10 customers never returned. In contrast, 46% of customers of the Carphone Warehouse "browse and buy" mobile shop bought more than one item of content, either in the same session or in later sessions (source: Bango).

Put simply, "browse and buy" leads to multiple purchases and increased profits.

In fact, "browse and buy" could be the subtitle for this book. In these pages we'll show you how to make an easy-to-use browsable mobile internet site, and how to help people to buy from you. Charging for access to content is fast and easy using the services provided by Bango.

## How does Bango fit in?

In its own words, Bango "enables the global marketplace for interactive mobile content". In essence Bango performs three deceptively simple tasks:

- **Effective promotion**: Bango enables you to promote your mobile internet content in a number of highly effective and simple ways.
- **Universal charging**: Bango lets you charge users for access to that content, wherever the content's stored and wherever the users are.
- **Easy navigation**: Bango allows users to navigate to your content in a number of straightforward and easy-to-use ways.

Bango takes care of all the difficult parts—identifying users, integrating with the billing systems of network operators, handling currency exchanges, accepting multiple methods of payment including credit/debit cards, and more—and lets you get on with providing new and interesting content and keeping your customers satisfied. Bango also provides a number of methods to help you promote your site, check your revenue and spot trends in time to exploit them. And Bango works closely with the industry to ensure that parents and guardians can control access to adult or violent content.

Of course Bango is in business to make money. It does so in two main ways: Bango customers pay a monthly subscription for the Bango Service (there are different rates, as we'll see); and it also takes a small slice of the income from its customers' sites. This approach ensures that Bango works hard to keep its customers happy: only by growing its customers' businesses can Bango itself grow.

The products and services described here are correct at time of going to press. Bango is constantly improving its services, so you may find some differences if you decide to sign up. We aim to update this book regularly to keep pace with the changes.

The Bango Service enables you to:

- Develop a revenue-generating mobile internet site.
- Provide users with easy access to the site through any marketing channel.
- Apply flexible pricing in pounds, euros and dollars.
- Bill users around the world.
- Maximise your conversion rate of visitors to paying customers.
- Track and monitor usage and spending patterns in real time.
- Exploit affiliate and co-marketing opportunities.
- Ensure continuous 24/7 service coverage.
- Comply with ICSTIS and mobile operator content policies.

Bango also provides a simple personal home page where users can see the sites they have visited, keep track of their favourite sites, and send links to the best sites to their friends.

## Using Bango to make money

Here's an overview of the money-making process.

Bango sells a number of *packages*. Each package is bundled with a different range of features and quality of service: the more you pay (it's a monthly subscription), the more you get. As part of a package you receive some *Bango Numbers*—these are the tokens you use to charge for content, and also to promote your site. We'll describe the different packages and types of Bango Number in Chapter 7, and walk you through the sign-up process.

You log in to the Bango Members' Lounge web site, http://bango.com/members, to define how much to charge for, and where to find, the content associated with each Bango Number. Then you simply insert those Bango Numbers into your site in the appropriate places.

Next you promote your site. You could use the Bango Txt Trigger Service, which gives you an easy-to-explain way to bring people to your site with money to spend. This service uses short text messages in conjunction with Bango Numbers. You can also use the Bango Web Trigger Service, which lets you use your web site to push people to your mobile site quickly and easily.

As your site grows in popularity and your customers start buying your content, you begin to receive revenue. You can use the Members' Lounge to track exactly how much money you're making.

You can use your revenue to expand, buying more Bango Numbers to add to your package or even new packages. As your site grows you might choose to buy Bango Relay or Bango Identifier functionality for one or more of your Bango Numbers to add more advanced features to your site.

The chapters that follow give you full details of the process, and start you on your way to a successful, profitable mobile internet business.

Part II
# Creating your site

In this part of the book we'll show you how to put together your money-making mobile internet site from scratch.

You'll learn some simple WML, which is the language you use to describe mobile internet pages. Then you'll start to add content—first free content, then content your customers will need to pay to access. We'll explain how to restrict access to content that's not suitable for everyone.

We'll finish this part by describing the Bango Relay Service and Bango Identifier Service, which are the keys to enhancing and growing your site—and increasing your revenue—and how you can protect your content from unauthorised access.

This part of the book is aimed primarily at a technical audience. Read this if you're **implementing** the mobile internet site.

Chapter 4
# Introducing WML

WML is one of the languages you can use to create pages for your mobile internet site—the equivalent of web pages you see on your PC or Mac. We'll concentrate on WML (version 1.1, to be specific) in this book as it's the most widespread language currently in use—you'll be able to reach more paying customers using WML today than using any of the other languages.

In this chapter we'll cover only the most important parts of WML 1.1, the bits you need to get started and get earning! Don't worry if you've never heard of WML until now—it's not too difficult to pick up, and we'll include numerous examples here that you can copy and modify for your own use.

## What is WML?

WML stands for *Wireless Markup Language*. A *markup language* is just a fancy name for a system for describing information using special tags: in this case, an opening tag before the information, and a closing tag after the information (we describe this in detail below).

WML uses the tagging rules defined by XML (eXtensible Markup Language), which is increasingly used across the internet to encode information. In common with all popular *XML applications*, as they're called, WML has a well-defined set of tags that can be combined in well-defined ways. All phones that understand WML know what those tags are, and have built-in rules for turning those tags into what you see on the screen.

If the final result is a meal, then WML is a recipe, and XML is a set of rules for writing recipes.

## WML compared to other markup languages

WML is similar to HTML, the language used to define web pages viewed on your PC or Mac. However, HTML has slightly different tagging rules—it's not based on XML but on an older web-unfriendly system called SGML.

As the internet moves more towards XML, more browsers—including those on mobile devices—will start to support an XML-based version of HTML called XHTML. But for now, it's best to stick with WML for greatest compatibility with today's phones.

## WML and WAP

WML is often mentioned in the same breath as WAP, the Wireless Application Protocol. This is more fancy talk. All you need to know is that a WAP-enabled phone uses its WAP settings to connect to the same old internet you surf from your desk.

It's also good to know that the Mobile Data Association, which you would expect to be over-optimistic when predicting how WAP would grow in popularity, in fact underestimated its growth. The MDA's forecast of 13 billion WAP page impressions for the whole of 2004 was overtaken in November of that year, reaching an impressive 13.3 billion page impressions in total. For 2005, the MDA forecasts a total of 15 billion page impressions by the year's end.

## Differences between the mobile and fixed internet

WML pages are like web pages, and a WAP phone is like a web browser. On your phone, you select a link or type in a URL. The phone connects through the WAP gateway to the internet, fetches the WML file you asked for, and displays it. Just like the way the "traditional" web works. But there are a few differences:

- WML isn't as flexible as HTML. Mobile internet sites can't contain all the bells and whistles of today's web sites.

- On the web, most people have the same browser—Microsoft Internet Explorer, running on a PC. Other browsers are available—like Mozilla, Opera and Safari—but they're the minority. On the mobile internet, there's much more variety. Phones from different manufacturers all support WML, but they might not all display things the same way. In particular, downloadable files—like ringtones and graphics—need to be tailored to the phone or manufacturer.

- A single WML file can hold more than one WML page. In HTML, each page is stored in its own file. The WML approach lets phones download several related pages at once, which improves responsiveness for users: selecting a link in one page would display the other page straight away, with no network access.

# Tagging basics

WML uses XML rules for tagging. Here's a quick guide that skips over many of the tricky areas but tells you enough to get started. You'll find detailed tutorials for XML and XML-based languages on the web, and in other books.

If you already know HTML but don't know XML, it's still worth reading this section—there are important differences between the two.

## Start and end tags

In XML (and so in WML), to tag something you use a start tag, for example `<p>`, then the stuff you want to tag, and then the end tag, which is like the start tag but with a slash: `</p>`. For example:

```
<p>The quick brown fox</p>
```

Here the text `The quick brown fox` has been tagged with p. In XML terms, p is an *element*. It's one of the defined WML tags, in this case the tag that marks a paragraph. (This is deliberately like HTML: WML shares many tags with that language.)

If you know HTML: you can't leave out end tags in XML. They're mandatory.

## Attributes

Start tags (but not end tags) can include additional information. This is represented by *attributes*, as in this example:

```
<p align="center">The quick brown fox</p>
```

Here the attribute `align` is given the value `center`. Note the American spelling! The attribute applies to everything within the element: in this case, you'd see a centred paragraph. You can have many attributes within the same start tag, all in the form `name="value"`, each separated by spaces.

You can't include tags within attribute values. Attributes are usually used for simple types of data—one value from a set (such as `left`, `right`, `center`) or numbers from a range. If you need to include a double quote within an attribute value, you can surround the entire attribute value with single quotes instead. (If you want to include both types of quote within your value, one type of quote will need to be represented by an entity: see below.)

If you know HTML: you must quote attribute values, using single quotes or double quotes. You can't leave out the quotes.

## Nested tags

You can nest tags—include tags within tags. This example would make the word "fox" appear in bold type:

`<p align="center">The quick brown <b>fox</b></p>`

You can only nest tags if the rules of WML allow it. For example, you can't include a paragraph within another paragraph, so you can't include a p tag within another p tag.

## Empty tags

Some elements don't enclose anything. For example, in WML the `timer` element defines a timer that ticks down until something happens. There's nothing to tag, as the duration of the timer is defined using an attribute, so you use a special *self-closing* start tag:

`<timer value="30"/>`

The trailing slash makes it self-closing. This has exactly the same meaning as a start tag followed immediately by a end tag, with nothing between. You can use either approach—but the self-closing tag is preferred as it results in smaller files.

If you know HTML: self-closing tags don't exist in HTML.

## Entities

An *entity* is a sequence of characters that stands for another character (or sequence of characters). For example, since the < character always indicates the start of a tag, you use an entity if you *really* want a < character: in this case, you'd put &lt; (the lt means "less than").

Entities start with an ampersand, &. Then there's a short word naming the entity, with a final semi-colon ;.

Defined WML entities are:

| Entity | Meaning |
|--------|---------|
| &lt;   | <       |
| &gt;   | >       |
| &amp;  | &       |
| &quot; | "       |
| &apos; | '       |
|   | Non-breaking space |
| &shy;  | Discretionary (soft) hyphen |

You can use entities anywhere within tagged data and attribute values.

## A simple "Hello World!" WML file

Now we'll build up elements, entities and attributes into a complete WML file. We'll start with a simple example: a single WML page that displays "Hello World!". Here it is:

```
<?xml version="1.0"?>
<!DOCTYPE wml PUBLIC "-//WAPFORUM//DTD WML 1.1//EN"
   "http://www.wapforum.org/DTD/wml_1.1.xml">

<wml>
 <card id="helloworld" title="WML demo">
  <p align="center">Hello, World!</p>
 </card>
</wml>
```

Chapter 4 — Introducing WML

As with all the examples, you can type the file in yourself using a text editor such as Windows Notepad (don't use word processor programs, unless you make sure you save the file as plain text without formatting). Always save the file with the extension `.wml`, for example `hello.wml`.

Let's dissect the file section by section.

```
<?xml version="1.0"?>
<!DOCTYPE wml PUBLIC "-//WAPFORUM//DTD WML 1.1//EN"
    "http://www.wapforum.org/DTD/wml_1.1.xml">
```

The first line identifies the file as XML: it's the *XML declaration*. The ? symbols are necessary: see the XML specification for more on this.

The next two lines also don't resemble markup we've discussed before. These lines identify the *XML document type*: they tell your customers' phones (or in fact, any XML-aware browser) that what follows is WML version 1.1.

In your own site, always include these lines at the start of each file.

```
<wml>
    ...
</wml>
```

Following the declarations, we now start working from the outside in— following the nesting of the tags. First we see the "outer layer" of the WML file: starting and closing `wml` tags. Again, always include these tags, and don't put anything after the closing tag.

```
<card id="helloworld" title="WML demo">
    ...
</card>
```

Inside the `wml` element we see a `card` element. A card defines a single page: it's the equivalent of a web page. WML allows you up to six related cards in the same file: these simply have more `card` elements, after the first one (and all inside the `wml` element).

In WML terminology, all the cards in a single file make up a *deck*. Decks— files—should be no more than 2 KB in size for greatest compatibility.

In this example, the card has two attributes: `id`, with value `helloworld`, and `title`, with value `WML demo`. The `id` is important when you want to add links between cards and decks—each card within a deck must have a different value for `id`. The `title` is typically displayed at the top of the phone's screen.

```
<p align="center">Hello, World!</p>
```

Finally, within the card we see the content of the page. This will be displayed in the main part of the phone's screen, horizontally central.

## Publishing your WML file on the mobile internet

If you already have your own web site, it's simple:

1. Decide where to put the file on your web site. You can put it anywhere you want that's accessible by URL.

2. Make sure the web server is configured to use the appropriate MIME type for .wml files: text/vnd.wap.wml, and automatically delivers index.wml files instead of directory listings. See Appendix 2 for more information.

If you don't have a web site yet, it's not too difficult to set one up. Many companies sell internet hosting services with a range of features—and a range of prices to match. The best advice is to shop around for the deal that suits your needs.

Free hosting providers are also available, such as Yahoo! GeoCities (geocities.yahoo.com). With this service, you must sign up for a Yahoo! ID (if you use Yahoo! Messenger for instant messaging, you already have one). With GeoCities you receive 15 MB of disk space for your files—more than enough for small sites—and a URL of the form http://www.geocities.com/your-yahoo-id. However, you're restricted to 3 GB of data transfer per month. In the longer term, a paid-for web site—from Yahoo! or any other provider—would be a good investment.

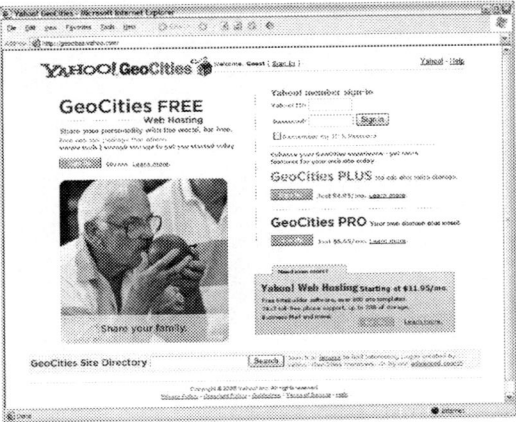

After you receive your Yahoo! ID and sign up to GeoCities, you'll see a page of options for building your site. At time of writing, the best way to set up a GeoCities WAP site is to create your WML files on your PC or Mac, and then upload them to your GeoCities site. Look for "Easy upload" in the Geocities "Advanced Toolbox" section.

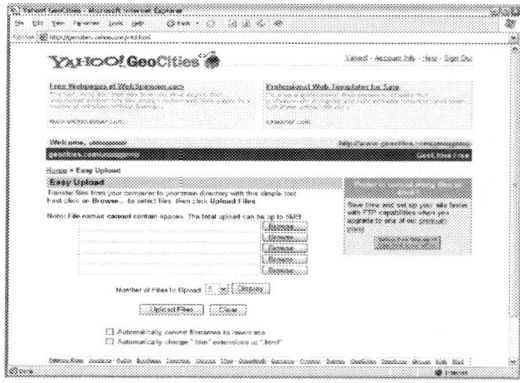

For the "Hello World!" example, try uploading to the top-level of your GeoCities account. Assuming you named the file hello.wml, this has the URL http://www.geocities.com/your-yahoo-id/hello.wml.

Now try it out! On your phone, start up a WAP session and go to your GeoCities "Hello World!" URL. You should see something like this:

If you use another hosting provider, you should see much the same thing. If you receive an error, the most likely cause is that the hosting provider hasn't configured their web site to support WML files. It's an easy change for them to make: get in touch with them and ask. You can find details of the configuration required in Appendix 2.

That's the hard part done. The rest of this part of the book just builds on top of knowledge gained here.

## "Hello again, World!": adding links and images

A single WML file that says "Hello World!" won't make you much money. The next step is to add links and images, to allow customers to move between pages, and to make the pages visually more appealing.

For this example we'll add a new card to our deck which contains an image. We'll also modify the first card so that the "Hello World!" text is a link to the second card. Here's the result (call it hello2.wml):

```
<?xml version="1.0"?>
<!DOCTYPE wml PUBLIC "-//WAPFORUM//DTD WML 1.1//EN"
  "http://www.wapforum.org/DTD/wml_1.1.xml">

<wml>
 <card id="helloworld" title="WML demo">
  <p align="center"><a href="#worldimage">Hello, World!</a></p>
 </card>
 <card id="worldimage" title="The World">
  <p align="center"><img src="world.gif" alt="World"/></p>
 </card>
</wml>
```

You'll notice how the second card slots into the file just after the first, and has a different id.

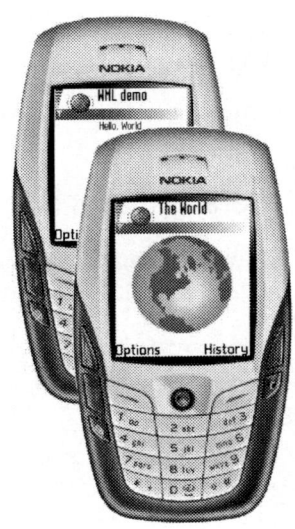

To create a link between the two cards, we've tagged the "Hello World!" text with a new element, a. This works in the same way as the HTML a element. This element has an href (hypertext reference) attribute with the URL of the destination of the link. In this case, we're linking within the same deck, so we use a within-file URL: the # symbol followed by the ID of the card we're linking to.

You can use any URL within an href attribute. Examples include:

- file.wml—to link to another deck
- file.wml#card—to link to a card within another deck
- directory/file.wml—to link to a deck within a subdirectory of the current directory

- `../file.wml`—to link to a deck one level up within the directory structure.
- `http://www.example.com/directory/file.wml`—to link to a deck on another site.

In the second card, we've used the `img` element to refer to an image called `world.gif` (in this example, in the same directory as the `hello2.wml` file). Notice that this is a self-closing tag: there's nothing within the element except two attributes, so there's no need for a separate closing tag. (The `src` attribute is just like `href`—the value can be any URL. The `alt` attribute displays text as an alternative to the image—some phones, such as the Nokia 3650, will refuse to display a page if an image doesn't have alternative text defined in this way.)

By adding an image, we've introduced a potential incompatibility: not all phones will be able to display this image. For example, older monochrome phones don't support the GIF image format used in this example—they may only support the two-colour WBMP, or wireless bitmap, format. Most new phones have colour screens and can display GIF images. Many phones can also display images in JPEG format.

It's important to be careful with image file sizes, since some phones won't load files that are too big (and sadly, each phone has its own idea of what's "too big" and what's not).

See Appendix 1 for device compatibility information.

## Timers and events

For our last example in this chapter, we'll demonstrate some WML aspects that don't have direct equivalents in HTML: timers and events.

In this example—call it `hello3.wml`—we'll add a timer. If the user doesn't select the link within five seconds, the phone automatically displays the second card.

```
<?xml version="1.0"?>
<!DOCTYPE wml PUBLIC "-//WAPFORUM//DTD WML 1.1//EN"
  "http://www.wapforum.org/DTD/wml_1.1.xml">

<wml>
 <card id="helloworld" title="WML demo" ontimer="#worldimage">
  <timer value="50"/>
```

```
    <p align="center"><a href="#worldimage">Hello, World!</a></p>
  </card>
  <card id="worldimage" title="The World">
    <p align="center"><img src="world.gif" alt="World"/></p>
  </card>
</wml>
```

The only changes from `hello2.wml` are an `ontimer` attribute within the first `card` element, and a new, empty `timer` element.

The `timer` element causes a internal clock to start ticking on the phone when the enclosing card is displayed. When the clock reaches 50 tenths of a second—five seconds—something gets triggered. This is called an *event*. In this case, the "something" is defined by the `ontimer` attribute, which tells the phone to go to the URL specified—the second card.

## Hints and tips

If you're not comfortable writing WML files by hand, online web editing tools are available: for example, Peperoni (www.mcommunity.biz) and TagTag (tagtag.com). They can help you build your web site relatively quickly and easily, and include tools for converting text and pictures into WML. Be aware, though, that they're limited to creating simple sites.

When writing WML files by hand, there are two golden rules:

- Keep it short.
- Keep it small.

Mobile phones typically only have a few lines on which to display text. Even the larger screens on the newer smartphones can't be compared favourably to the average PC. Keep the text you write as short as possible.

The second rule is related to the first: it's important to keep the physical file sizes as small as you can. This improves download speed for the files, if only by a little, but also improves compatibility since many phones have strict limits on file sizes. The Sony Ericsson T68i, for example, doesn't support decks greater than 3000 bytes in size—so your WML files must be less than 3 KB to support that phone.

Actually, there's a platinum rule that's more important than the two golden rules combined: **Test your site out on as many phones as you can.** There's more on compatibility and testing in the next chapter.

## Summary

This chapter has only covered the basics of WML: how to create your first mobile internet pages, with simple links, images and timers. The full WML language has many more features, such as support for variables (which can be passed between cards in a deck) and forms (to let people input data for processing).

If you're interested in learning about these features, a good source for more WML information is W3 Schools (www.w3schools.com). There you'll find a complete WML tutorial and reference, with more examples.

In the next chapter we'll show you how to create well-structured mobile internet sites: the crucial next step towards making money.

# Chapter 5
# Structuring your mobile internet site

In the previous chapter we introduced you to WML, a language for defining mobile internet sites in terms of decks and cards. Now we'll take a step back and look at the overall structure of your site. What are the best tactics for structuring your site to maximise your revenue?

Here's an overview of a typical well-organised site:

- A simple home page with small logo and links to major site sections.
- One section for each content category.
- New, popular and free content prominently labelled.
- Prices of paid-for content clearly shown.
- Content available in every category that makes sense.
- Thumbnail images or teaser text for free and paid content.

## The home page

Your (potential) customers are visiting with a simple goal: to access any interesting content you might have. Make sure your home page tells them what they need to know. Your home page is your shopfront: it's where you show off your wares, tempt customers to buy, and demonstrate how up-to-date you are.

A common mistake is to make a home page show a logo for a few seconds then move to a separate page. Some people believe that this reinforces their brand image. In fact it does the opposite. Your business exists to sell content, not to promote itself. Your customers visit to buy content, not to admire the curves of your logo. Show your logo by all means, but make it a part—a small part—of your home page.

With very limited screen space on most mobile phones there's no room for redundant text. You don't need to welcome your visitors to the site or wish them good morning. A simple tag line that communicates your business message is all you need to accompany your logo. For example, "News & Pics—25x7" conveys in just a few words everything you need to know about the style, attitude and purpose of a gossip site.

We recommend you follow your tag line with clearly written links to each section of the site, indicating which sections have been updated recently. You don't need any more text on your home page, though you might want to include a short copyright notice at the bottom of the page.

Your home page is important as it gives customers a well-signposted route into your valuable content. Make sure every page on your site links back to the home page: this makes it easy for customers to find more of your content.

## Sections of your site

How you split your site into sections depends very much on the content that you're giving access to. The best approach is to think like a customer: if *you* were visiting the site, where would *you* look for something?

One idea for figuring out a good structure is to buy a box of 3x5 cards and write, on each one, the title and description of a piece of content that you intend to sell. Then find some willing members of your target audience—or some friends, though the results might not be as good—and ask them in turn (and away from everyone else) to organise the cards into groups. Write down the results for each person, and shuffle the cards before giving them to the next person.

You might find that everyone has grouped the cards differently, but the chances are you'll spot some common groupings. Use them—no matter how odd they seem to you. Your target market has spoken!

This approach to grouping is often used when designing and testing web sites, and is part of the much larger field of *usability*. Invest in a good usability book to learn more about this subject: your site usability directly affects your revenue.

What happens if half your test subjects group the cards one way, and the other half groups them another, contradictory way? For example, there might be a "group by Hollywood star" faction and a "group by type of content" faction. In this case you have two options: pick one or the other grouping strategy; or pick both.

There's nothing to stop a single piece of content appearing in more than one section. In fact, if you want to maximise revenue, you should put content wherever someone might reasonably look for it. Here are some ideas for this more flexible grouping strategy:

- Group by subject matter (who's in the content?)
- Group by type (what type of content is it?)
- Group by date (how new is the content?)
- Group by popularity (how many people have accessed the content?)
- Group by price (how much will it cost the customer to access?)

## New content

Regular new content helps bring back existing customers. It's crucial that these customers can find the new content easily. New content also helps new customers: it reassures them that the site is living and vibrant, and a good site to return to later.

Many sites have a prominent "What's new" link on their home page. (This is another way of saying "group by date" as described in the previous section.) You should also make sure every piece of content added recently is also labelled as new. It's up to you how you define "recent"—often, content is labelled new until the next new content arrives, or simply for a fixed period after it first appears.

In long lists of content such as an index of news articles, it's best to put new content at the top (unless the lists are specifically sorted another way, for example alphabetically).

## Popular content

Nobody likes to look unfashionable, unless being unfashionable is the current fashion. Consequently many sites highlight the most popular content, usually with a prominent "Top Ten" link from the home page (it's the "group by popularity" method described above).

Top tens can increase revenue simply because people like to "follow the crowd". But they also help you spot trends more quickly. If more people are reading gossip articles about a new film star, then adding more content related to the film star—images, videos, or more text articles—could well be a moneyspinner.

## Loss leaders: free content

In business terms, a loss leader is something you sell (or give away) for less than its true value in the hope that this will attract customers to your business—and your other, more fairly priced products. A good example is a games console: consoles are often sold for less than they cost to build, with the money recouped from sales of the games themselves.

The best way to make use of loss leaders in your mobile internet site is to give away free samples: demonstrate to your potential customers the quality of your content. As long as your free samples are good enough, you should attract paying customers. You should make sure your free samples are prominently labelled on your site: consider putting them in their own section, available direct from the home page.

Sites that sell images (for customers to use as background images on their phone, for example) often give away free samples modified to include their site name prominently across the image. This lets them sell the unmodified originals as well as demonstrate image quality to their potential customers.

Be careful not to give away too many free samples! One or two of each type should be enough.

# Thumbnails and teasers

When was the last time you bought something sight unseen? It's unlikely that many people will spend money, even a small amount, without having a good idea of what they'll receive. For that reason, your mobile internet sites should include thumbnails or teasers—small snippets of the full content.

A *thumbnail* is a small, sometimes cropped version of an image. A good thumbnail shows enough of the complete image to give the potential purchaser a reason to buy, without being valuable itself. If you make your thumbnails too big, potential customers might just copy the thumbnail rather than pay for the image. But if you make it too small, it will turn into a smudge. A rough guide (a rule of thumb?) for phone thumbnails is to make them about one-quarter to one-third the width and height of the full image. You can use thumbnail images for games and videos, too: include a smaller image of the game in action, or an exciting or teasing still from the video.

A *teaser* is a sample, such as the introduction, of a piece of text or music. Good written teasers hook the reader into wanting more by hinting at the content of the full story. Good musical teasers give a flavour of the full piece but lack crucial parts, such as a complete melody.

For ideas on what works and examples of successful mobile sites, visit www.bango.com.

Chapter 6
# Building a free-content site

In this chapter we'll build on the knowledge of the previous two chapters to create a complete site including content. (For now, the content will be free for anyone to access.) By content we mean any self-contained item of value that can be placed on the mobile internet. It could be a ringtone, an image, a video, a game, or even just text such as a news article, a list of items or an up-to-date price quote.

We'll start with what should be two of your principal concerns when you develop your site: phone compatibility and testing.

## Phone compatibility

As we explained in Chapter 4, the mobile internet has much more variety than the fixed internet. There are many different types of phones, with different abilities and restrictions. Unfortunately for you, the content provider, you have to think carefully about which types of phone you want to support. The more phones you support, the more content you'll need to provide, tailored to each phone.

Potential incompatibilities:

- Some phones support polyphonic ringtones, others only monophonic. Supported ringtone file formats differ between different phone vendors.
- Most of today's colour phones support GIF image formats, but not all phones support JPEG images. Some support PNG or TIFF images. Some phones can display more colours than others.
- Fewer phones support videos, and there's more than one video format.
- Some phones support Java or BREW-based applications, some don't.

- Not all phones support WML in exactly the same way. You might find that different phones display the same WML file in different ways. For example, some phones support WML tables correctly, but others don't.

At first glance this may look like an insurmountable problem. How on earth can you make sure your customers receive the right content? The good news is that this is a well-known problem: many others have trodden the path before you. The bad news is that you still have to do some work yourself. To find out how you can determine the capabilities of different phones, see Appendix 1.

## Testing your site

The information in Appendix 1 helps you produce content suitable for different phones, but theory is no substitute for practice. It's important to test your site with as many different models of phone as you can.

You may want to consider a session at Bango's test centre, which has a large range of popular phones. Contact Bango for more information.

If you don't use Bango's test centre, then ask your friends, your family, your colleagues, people you meet in the street, anyone. The more you test, the more opportunities you'll have to fix problems before your potential customers find them.

### Functional and usability testing

Broadly speaking there are two areas your tests should cover:

- **Functionality: does the site work as it should?** Do the correct pages appear? Do your graphics display properly? Does the downloadable content work for all phones you want to support?
- **Usability: is the site as easy-to-use as possible?** Can your customers find your content easily? Is it clear how to download the content? (See Chapter 5 for tips on structuring your site.)

It's worth investing the time to write a *test plan* before you visit the Bango test centre (or before you ask your friends to help). While you might get useful results by just trying out the site and noting any problems, you'll get better results if you work out in advance what you want to test, and how you want to test it. For example, you probably want to make sure that all major parts of the site are tested on all phone types.

A test plan can be as simple as a printed checklist for each phone type. As well as a useful reminder of what to test, they're also good places to note down the results. Don't rely on memory—your own or your friends'—to put together a list of problems later.

If you're using friends to help test the site, a good way to test ease-of-use—or *usability*—is to give your friends a list of tasks to complete. For example, "Download the gossip article about Star Wars". Don't tell them how to complete the task: just watch them try, and don't help or even speak while they're attempting the task. Remember: your real customers won't have you there to assist them. If your friends can't complete a task, you have a usability problem. Think about how you can change the site to make it easier to use.

At the time of writing, a web search for "usability" returns nearly three million hits. Plenty of sites to check for more testing tips!

## "Free Hollywood"—a complete site

Let's imagine we're putting together a mobile internet site about Hollywood, devoted to bringing the latest gossip and photos to a mobile audience. We have two types of content: text and images. For now, all the content's free to access. We're happy to write WML pages, but we don't want to start writing programs.

In this section we'll describe a suitable structure for this site, which we'll call "Free Hollywood", and some of the pages in detail. You can use this site as a starting point for your own site, if you want: all files are available at http://examples.bango.net/freehollywood.zip.

> **Try it out now!**
> On your mobile phone, start an internet session and go to bango.net. In the box, type 3733465599663 (the phone spelling for "freehollywood") and then select Go There.

## Site structure

In Chapter 5 we discussed how to structure your site from the perspective of the user—how the site should appear to customers and potential customers. Here we cover the same problem, but from the perspective of the site developer—where to place the files and directories that make up the site.

Many people build sites organically: they start with a couple of files, discover a need for some more, and add them in a haphazard fashion. This is fine for very small sites. But when the site starts to grow, the content provider finds that managing the site becomes increasingly difficult. The haphazard arrangement isn't suited to larger sites—it doesn't scale.

To make an analogy with food: "A moment on the lips, a lifetime on the hips". Adding content wherever it fits is easy; rearranging it later so it makes sense is much harder. If you have any plans to grow your site beyond a few pages, then start thinking about how you want that larger site to look before you start creating anything. You'll be glad you did.

For our Free Hollywood site we'll plan for a reasonable amount of growth, and structure the site accordingly. Here's an outline:

- At the top level of the site there's an `index.wml` file. This deck contains two cards: the home page of the site, and the feedback page. At this level we'll also store the Hollywood site logo, `hollywood.gif`

- Also at the top level, alongside the home page, are a number of subdirectories. Using subdirectories helps to keep the site clean and uncluttered, and therefore more manageable.

- Inside subdirectories called `gossip` and `gallery` we'll store index files—cards that link to text and image content, respectively.

- Inside `releases` will be one or more files listing upcoming movie releases. (In this example we don't consider this information content, just a useful service for customers.)

- Inside `content` we'll store the content itself. (Why put all content in one place, rather than inside the `gossip` and `gallery` directories? Imagine we wanted later to add sections for particular Hollywood stars, including both gossip and images related to each star. Keeping the section indexes independent of the content makes this easier to manage.)

- Each file—whether an index file or a file containing content—has a strict *naming convention*. In other words, the content provider has laid down rules for filenames to make management easier.

The naming conventions are:

- Within `gossip` and `releases` (both used for index files), the most recent index is always called `index.wml`. Older index files include numbers in the filename, with the oldest index called `01_index.wml`. When we need a new index file, we rename the current `index.wml` to the next number in the sequence, say `23_index.wml`, and create a new `index.wml` for the new index. (We use this approach so that the home page only ever needs to link to the `index.wml` file in each subdirectory—always the latest index. More usefully for the business, this also means that customers can bookmark `index.wml` to jump straight to the index for the newest content.)

- Within `gallery` a similar rule applies, except we've decided to maintain separate indexes for pictures of men and women. So the file `index.wml` in this directory just links to the separate male and female indexes, `men.wml` and `women.wml`. Older gender-specific index files are numbered as above, for example `05_men.wml`.

- Within `content` we're storing all content. Text content uses standard WML files. For images, we'll need the downloadable image (in GIF format) and a thumbnail (also in GIF, displayed on a gallery index page). We'll give each item of content a number and a short description (for example, `04_cage`). For thumbnails we'll add `_th`. Then we'll use the standard file extension to distinguish between GIF and WML files.

This is less complicated in practice than it might appear in theory! Naming conventions are designed to make filenames predictable and easy to understand, so that content providers don't need to know the structure intimately to modify or add a file. To illustrate this, here's the structure of our Hollywood site in full (after a few months, when there's enough content for multiple indexes):

```
index.wml
hollywood.gif
content
—01_berry.wml
—02_epzero.wml
—03_streep.wml
```

```
—04_cage.wml
—05_sign.wml
—06_lynda.gif
—06_lynda_th.gif
—07_steve.gif
—07_steve_th.gif
—etc
gallery
—index.wml
—men.wml
—women.wml
—01_men.wml
—02_men.wml
—01_women.wml
—02_women.wml
—03_women.wml
gossip
—index.wml
—01_index.wml
—02_index.wml
releases
—index.wml
—01_index.wml
```

In our site structure we've planned for up to a hundred items of content, and a hundred indexes of each type. This is plenty for this type of site. If your site grows as large as this or larger, then you'll want to invest in a more flexible way of building your site and charging for content. We'll talk more about this in Chapter 7 and Chapter 9.

In sections that follow we'll work through some of the files on the Free Hollywood site. As the pattern should soon become obvious, we won't describe each and every file—but don't forget you can download all the files from `http://examples.bango.net/freehollywood.zip` to examine them in more detail if you want.

## The home and feedback cards

The top-level `index.wml` file is a deck containing two files: the home page and the feedback page. Here it is in full:

```
<?xml version="1.0"?>
<!DOCTYPE wml PUBLIC "-//WAPFORUM//DTD WML 1.1//EN"
  "http://www.wapforum.org/DTD/wml_1.1.xml">

<wml>
```

```
<card id="home" title="Hollywood">
 <p align="center"><img src="hollywood.gif" alt="Hollywood" vspace="0" hspace="0"/><br/>
 News &amp; Pics - 25x7<br/>
 <a href="gossip/index.wml">Latest gossip</a> (Mar 13)<br/>
 <a href="releases/index.wml">New releases</a> (Mar 10)<br/>
 <a href="gallery/index.wml">Picture gallery</a> (Mar 10)<br/>
 <a href="#contact">Contact us</a></p>
</card>

<card id="contact" title="Contact us">
 <p>Psst - got gossip? Any news to spread? Some dirt to dish?</p>

 <p>If so, get in touch! Send it to <b>gossip@example.com</b> - mystery
 star prize for the best gossip each month...</p>
</card>
</wml>
```

New elements and attributes:

- Within the img element: alt defines some text to display instead of the graphic (for example, while the graphic is loading); and vspace and hspace define how much vertical and horizontal space, in pixels, to include around the graphic.
- The br element causes a line break at that point.
- The b marks up text to be displayed in bold.

Some points to note:

- We're using the amp entity to display the & symbol.
- We're using line breaks to ensure each link starts on a new line on the phone screen.
- We're including dates to help our customers know when new content has arrived.
- The second card assumes that our customers will be able to send and receive email.
- We're offering our customers an incentive to send in more news.

## The gossip index

This is the file stored at `gossip/index.wml`, linked to from the home page. This file links to the most recent gossip.

```
<?xml version="1.0"?>
<!DOCTYPE wml PUBLIC "-//WAPFORUM//DTD WML 1.1//EN"
  "http://www.wapforum.org/DTD/wml_1.1.xml">

<wml>
 <card id="gossip" title="Latest gossip">

<p>Last update: Mar 13</p>

<p><a href="../content/05_sign.wml">Changes afoot for Hollywood sign</a><br/>
<a href="../content/04_cage.wml">Silent movies to make a comeback?</a><br/>
<a href="../content/03_streep.wml">Meryl plays the Joker</a><br/>
<a href="../content/02_epzero.wml">What's next after Episode 3 for Lucas?</a><br/>
<a href="../content/01_berry.wml">Berry declines Loo-crative role</a></p>

 <p><a href="../index.wml">Home</a></p>
 </card>
</wml>
```

Points to note:

- Customers see straight away when new content was last added. This helps customers who've bookmarked this page.

- The most recent link—the newest gossip—is at the top.

- We're using "teaser" text to entice the reader to select the link.

- We're linking back to the home page.

## Gossip content

This is the file stored at `content/02_epzero.wml`, linked to from the gossip index. This file is a piece of content: a gossip article.

```
<?xml version="1.0"?>
<!DOCTYPE wml PUBLIC "-//WAPFORUM//DTD WML 1.1//EN"
  "http://www.wapforum.org/DTD/wml_1.1.xml">

<wml>
  <card id="epzero" title="Pre-prequel">

<p><b>Yada yada Yoda</b>.
If you thought George Lucas was done with the Star Wars
universe, think again. No, it's not Episodes 7, 8 and 9.
Not even remakes of 4, 5 and 6. Yes, it's Episode Zero,
folks.</p>

<p>Casting producers worldwide be on alert. Sometime soon the
full might of Skywalker Ranch will be upturning every stone
in the hunt for teen Obi Wan. After the English original and
the Scottish prequel, what are the bets on a Welsh Kenobi this
time?</p>

<p>Story? Who cares, as long as we see Yoda fight again...</p>

<p><a href="../gossip/index.wml">Gossip</a><br/>
<a href="../index.wml">Home</a></p>
  </card>
</wml>
```

Points to note:

- There's not a lot of room on most phones to display the card title. We're using it here almost as a teaser, or a summary of the gossip.

- We've chosen to include a "run-in heading" as a piece of bold text at the start of the first paragraph. All the gossip articles follow the same pattern: this helps reinforce a style and attitude for the entire site.

- The text is short and direct, reflecting the need to convey as much as possible on a small screen.

- As well as a link to the home page, we're also linking to the gossip index page.

Another thing we should mention, just in case: all the gossip articles on the Free Hollywood site are invented. None of the gossip is true—well, as far as we know!

## The male gallery index

This is the file stored at `gallery/men.wml`, linked to from the `gallery/index.wml` file. This file links to the most recent image content, and includes thumbnails.

```
<?xml version="1.0"?>
<!DOCTYPE wml PUBLIC "-//WAPFORUM//DTD WML 1.1//EN"
  "http://www.wapforum.org/DTD/wml_1.1.xml">

<wml>
 <card id="men" title="Men">

<p>Last update: Mar 9</p>

<p><a href="../content/13_dave.gif"><img src="../content/13_dave_th.gif" alt="Dave"/>Dave</a><br/>
<a href="../content/11_mike.gif"><img src="../content/11_mike_th.gif" alt="Mike"/>Mike</a><br/>
<a href="../content/09_chris.gif"><img src="../content/09_chris_th.gif" alt="Chris"/>Chris</a><br/>
<a href="../content/07_steve.gif"><img src="../content/07_steve_th.gif" alt="Steve"/>Steve</a></p>


  <p><a href="../index.wml">Home</a></p>
 </card>
</wml>
```

Points to note:

- We're linking to the content—the image file itself.
- The link surrounds both the description and the thumbnail image.

## Compatibility

The Free Hollywood site is simple enough that compatibility issues don't really arise. The content is delivered as relatively short text articles and small GIF images for maximum compatibility.

How would we change the site to support trickier types of content? Let's use the example of video content. The Nokia 3650 and 6600 models (and others) support both 3GPP and Real Media format for videos. However, the Sony Ericsson P800 only supports 3GPP.

In this case, we'd add a `video` directory (with index files arranged the same way as with `gossip`). Within these index files we'd include a thumbnail and link to a WML file in `content`. Within the WML file in `content` we'd link to both 3GPP and Real Media versions of the content—files named, for example, `15_cupgoal.3gp` and `15_cupgoal.rm`—making sure the links were labelled appropriately. The customer would need to choose the appropriate link for their device.

We could use the same technique to make Java or BREW-based games and "wallpaper" (phone screen background) images available for phones with different screen sizes. However, distributing wallpaper this way this could quickly become unwieldy due to the large number of different screen sizes available with today's phones.

In Chapter 7 we'll discuss how you can improve your customers' experience by only giving them access to content that's suitable for their phone. See also Appendix 1 for more on the different devices and the content they support.

## Summary

In this chapter we've shown how to create a simple free-content site very easily in WML. We've avoided too many compatibility issues, but we've emphasised the importance of this tricky area and how functional testing and usability testing can help us find bugs before our customers do.

In the next chapter we'll start to integrate Bango services with our site, turning free content into chargeable content.

Chapter 7
# Adding chargeable content using the Bango Service

In this chapter our site will start to earn money. We'll convert the "Free Hollywood" site from the last chapter into "Hollywood Reloaded"—almost identical, but using Bango services to charge customers for access to some content.

The Bango system uses *Bango Numbers* as alternatives to URLs. Put simply, you set up the Bango system to associate your Bango Number with your site (or a part of it) and a charge, and when a customer accesses your Bango Number they'll be charged that amount and then redirected to your site. Bango Numbers are included as part of the Bango *package* to which you subscribe. We'll see in this chapter how you integrate Bango Numbers into your mobile shop.

## Bango packages

As we outlined in Chapter 3, Bango sells a number of packages bundled with different features. Each package targets a different market segment:

- The *Pro* package is for large companies with lots of content, sophisticated delivery mechanisms and a requirement for a higher level of service with service guarantees.
- The *Focus* package is for medium-to-large companies with lots of content who want to provide a personalised mobile retail experience.
- The *Express* package is for small-to-medium companies with large amounts of content and more sophisticated delivery mechanisms.
- The *Micro* package is for small companies, hobbyists and those with small amounts of content to sell.

Each package is available for a monthly fee—for the latest prices please contact Bango or visit www.bango.com.

# Bango Numbers

A Bango Number is nothing magic: it's just a number, usually with a large number of digits. The magic lies in the association between the number, your content and you. The Bango system knows how much to charge when someone accesses your content using that number, and knows that you receive the appropriate slice of revenue as a result.

Bango uses easy-to-understand categories—Gold, Silver, Bronze and Standard—to describe different lengths of Bango Number:

- Gold numbers are 1-5 digits in length.
- Silver numbers have 6-7 digits.
- Bronze numbers have 8-9 digits.
- Standard numbers are 10-50 digits in length.

Each package gives you the right to choose some Bango Numbers, with the more expensive packages giving you more—and shorter—numbers. None of the packages bundles Gold Bango Numbers as standard—they're available only as add-ons.

If Bango Numbers are effectively just tokens, then why bother categorising them by length and giving shorter numbers to people who pay more? The reason is that Bango Numbers are used in two ways:

- **For internal use within your site.** These *internal numbers* are sometimes called *billing numbers* as they're primarily used to charge for access to content. But you can charge nothing if you want: as Bango gives you usage statistics for all your Bango Numbers, you can use free-to-access Bango Numbers to track visits to your site, or to particular sections or pages within the site. You don't care how long an internal Bango Number is, as your customers will never see it.

- **For access to your site.** These *access numbers* are Bango Numbers you use to promote your site. You want your access Bango Numbers to be as short as possible, as your customers will use them—or the "phone spelling" word form of them (see Chapter 15). See Chapter 13 for tips on choosing a suitable access Bango Number.

So the higher the value of the Bango package you subscribe to, the better access Bango Numbers you get to choose. You can choose any unallocated Bango Number you want within the categories available to you. When you sign up to the Bango Service the web pages will guide you through this process.

Bango packages also include *tracking* Bango Numbers. These are Standard-class but random numbers—you don't get to choose these—that you can use for any purpose. Due to their randomness they're most useful as internal numbers.

You can add more Bango Numbers to a package at any time.

With the Pro, Focus and Express packages you can designate some of your Bango Numbers to have Relay functionality; the Pro and Focus packages can assign Identifier functionality as well. These features, useful for large-content sites, are not available to purchasers of the Micro package—and can't be added later. See Chapter 9 and Chapter 10 for more information on these features.

## The Members' Lounge web site

In the lingo of the web, the Members' Lounge is the Bango customer portal. It's where you go to perform all tasks related to the Bango Service.

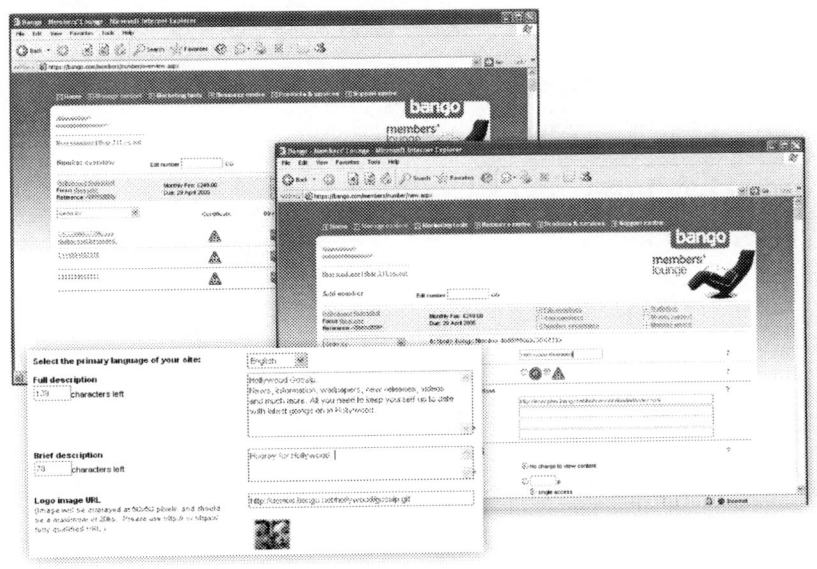

You can register to access the Members' Lounge for free: simply provide an email address, and Bango will send you a confirmation message that you can use to activate your access. Once registered you can log in at http://bango.com/members.

Within the Members' Lounge you can subscribe to a Bango package and select your Bango Numbers. Subscribers can then assign charges to Bango Numbers and associate them with your content, and then later check the revenue earned. You can access historical revenue information for trend analysis. You can also define your entries in the Bango Directory, and find additional marketing tools and support resources.

Note that although some parts of the Members' Lounge are open to all registered users, other information is only accessible to package subscribers.

## Buying a Bango package

Let's assume we want to buy the Focus package (the process is the same for the other packages). Here's what to do.

We start at the Bango home page by opening www.bango.com in a web browser. We can visit the "What's on Offer" section and read about the packages there before signing up. After choosing to sign up, during which we register an email address with Bango (there's a confirmation step to avoid fake registrations), we'll jump to the "Create a New Package" page of the Members' Lounge.

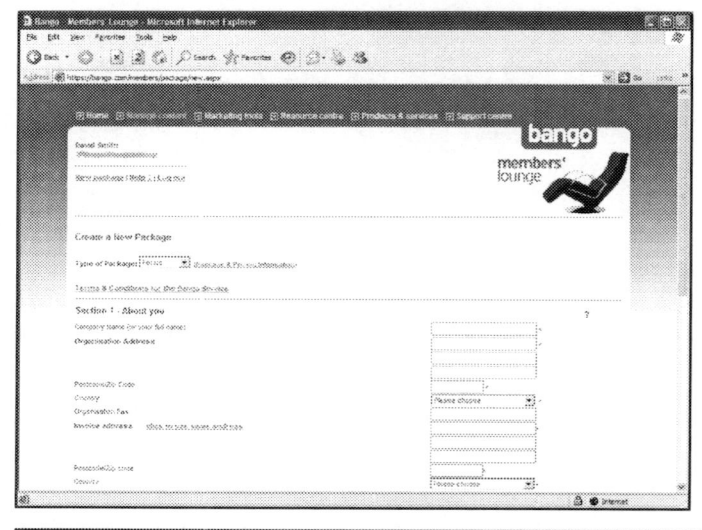

Now we fill in all the details. The Bango system gives different permissions to the people named as primary, support and finance contacts. For example, the finance contact can't change the content a Bango Number points to. Once we've finished this page we'll see a payment page that we can use to make the initial payment to Bango.

Once we've signed up we're taken to the Manage Content section of the Members' Lounge. This shows us everything about our package—not much right now! Next we need to start adding Bango Numbers.

To add a number, we just type it in the appropriate box. We can also type the word form in phone spelling of the number—the system automatically converts it for us. As we type, the category of number—Gold, Silver, Bronze or Standard—is highlighted. Finally we click Add Number to try to reserve that number as part of our package.

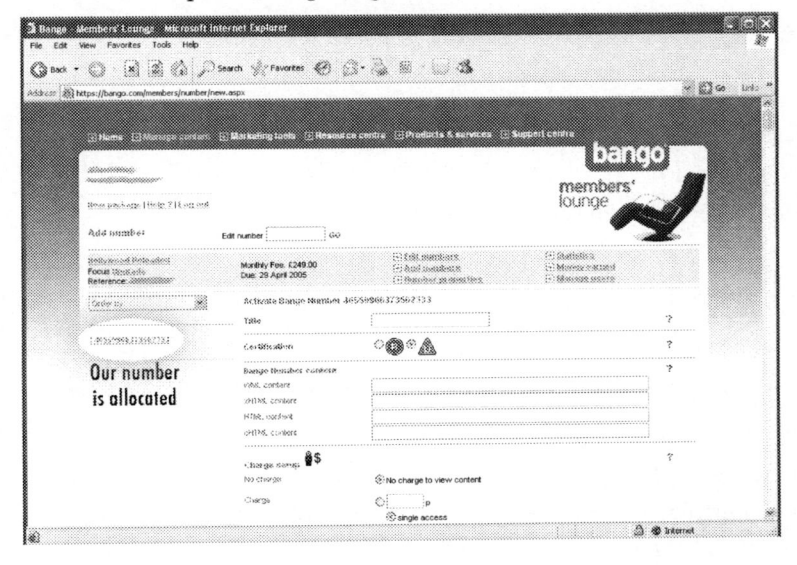

Chapter 7 — Adding chargeable content using the Bango Service

If nobody else is already using that Bango Number, as in this case, it's ours. (Notice we typed hollywoodreloaded in the box, and we've been allocated the phone spelling equivalent: 46559966373562333.)

We'll explain how to activate the Bango Numbers in the next section. For now we need to allocate two *tracking* numbers, which we'll use for billing purposes below. To allocate a tracking number, we click Add Numbers and simply click Add Tracking Number. Bango chooses tracking numbers automatically. We'll use two tracking numbers below, so in this example we follow this process twice.

Once both numbers are allocated, click Edit Numbers at the top to see a summary of all your Bango Numbers:

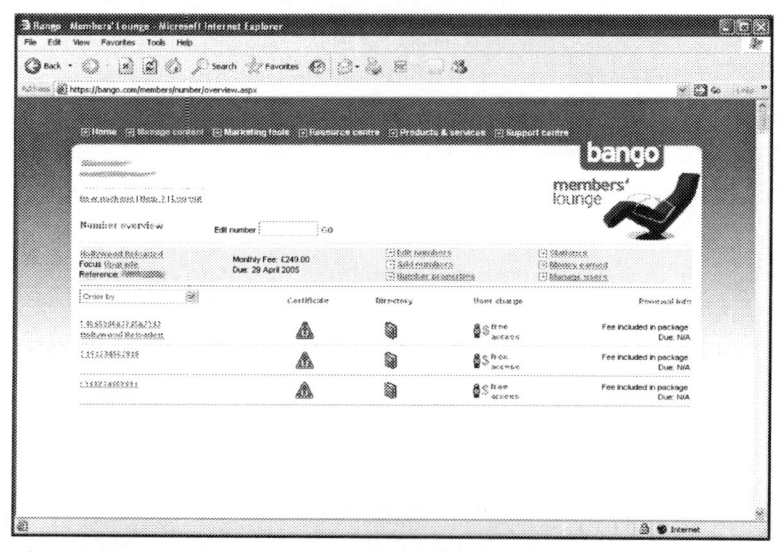

The Focus package has a generous bundle of Bango Numbers. But if we want more, we can add them by paying extra.

## "Hollywood Reloaded"

Now we've bought our Bango package and chosen our access and internal Bango Numbers, it's time to update our web site and make some content chargeable.

We're going to promote our access number, 46559966373562333, and want to link that to our home page at no charge. We'll use our other two numbers, 111234567910 and 111234567911, to charge for content. As we'll see, this means we can only charge for two pieces of content. (We can always buy more Bango Numbers to charge for other content.)

Let's charge 20p each for access to a recent gossip article (about the Hollywood sign) and a recent image (the picture of Dave).

## Mapping Bango Numbers to URLs and setting charges

Our first step is to associate our three Bango Numbers with the appropriate places on our site, and set the charges:

| Bango Number | URL | Charge |
|---|---|---|
| 46559966373562333 | http://examples.bango.net/hollywoodreloaded/index.wml | No charge |
| 111234567910 | http://examples.bango.net/hollywoodreloaded/content/05_sign.wml | 20p for single access |
| 111234567911 | http://examples.bango.net/hollywoodreloaded/content/13_dave.gif | 20p for single access |

To do this, we return to the Manage Content section of the Members' Lounge and edit each Bango Number in turn. The screenshot shows how it should look for our access number, 46559966373562333.

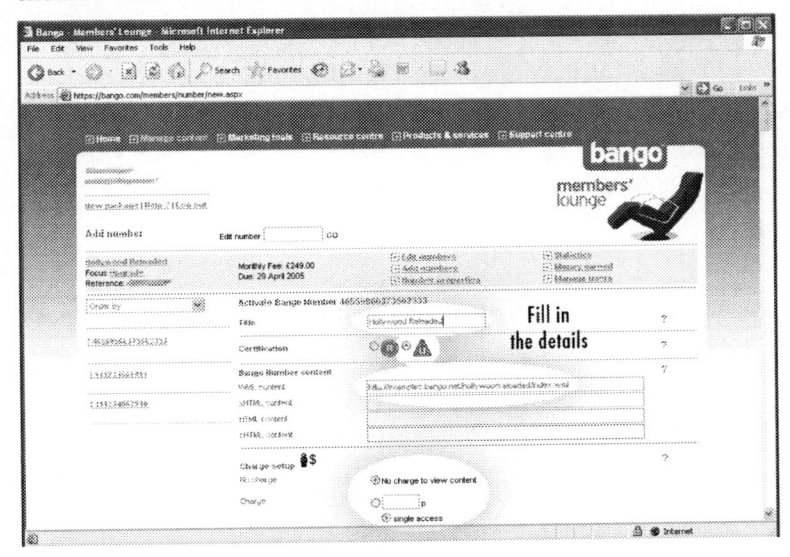

Chapter 7 – Adding chargeable content using the Bango Service

For each Bango Number, choose an appropriate title. This title is shown to your customers on payment screens. For the certification choose U (see Chapter 8 for help on restricting access to content).

Note that for each Bango Number we can define *four* URLs in the Bango Number Content section. The Bango system detects the type of device that a customer's using and chooses the most appropriate URL to redirect them to. For example, PC and Mac users would be redirected to the HTML URL. In this case we're only defining the WML URL.

Then we set the charge by selecting the appropriate option and typing the amount in the box. (See Chapter 18 for tips on how much to charge.)

Finally we ignore the Relay (see Chapter 9) and Directory (see Chapter 17) sections for now and click Activate Number.

We can now test out our site: on a WAP-enabled phone, go to the URL http://bango.net, type 46559966373562333 in the box, and select Go There. We should be redirected to the Hollywood Reloaded home page.

## Site changes

Now that we've defined charges and URLs for each of our Bango Numbers, it's a simple step to integrate Bango services into our site. Wherever we currently link to one of the chargeable URLs—here the gossip and image URLs we used in the previous section—we link to Bango's web site instead, including the appropriate Bango Number in the URL.

In our example we'll replace any references to the 05_sign.wml file with http://bango.net/111234567910, and references to 13_dave.gif with http://bango.net/111234567911.

Here's the resulting gossip index file for this site:

```
<?xml version="1.0"?>
<!DOCTYPE wml PUBLIC "-//WAPFORUM//DTD WML 1.1//EN"
   "http://www.wapforum.org/DTD/wml_1.1.xml">

<wml>
 <card id="gossip" title="Latest gossip">

<p>Last update: Mar 13</p>

<p><a href="http://bango.net/111234567910">Changes afoot for Hollywood sign</a><br/>
```

```
<a href="../content/04_cage.wml">Silent movies to make a
comeback?</a><br/>
<a href="../content/03_streep.wml">Meryl plays the Joker</
a><br/>
<a href="../content/02_epzero.wml">What's next after Episode 3
for Lucas?</a><br/>
<a href="../content/01_berry.wml">Berry declines Loo-crative
role</a></p>

 <p><a href="../index.wml">Home</a></p>
 </card>
</wml>
```

It's as simple as that. The site's now a potential money-earner!

We can try the site out on a mobile phone using ●46559966373562333.

As with "Free Hollywood" in Chapter 6, you can download the files that make up "Hollywood Reloaded" and use them as a starting point for your own site. Just remember to use your own Bango Numbers rather than the ones here! The files are available at http://examples.bango.net/hollywoodreloaded.zip.

## Typical user experience

Our site's a *potential* money-earner. What do our *potential* customers have to do to buy our chargeable content—to turn into *real* customers? Let's look at the typical user experience for buying content through Bango services.

We'll assume our potential customer, Mel, has never accessed any Bango service before now. She sees an advert for the Hollywood Reloaded site that tells her to text "go hollywoodreloaded" to 83055 ("hollywoodreloaded" is our access Bango Number, 46559966373562333 in phone spelling). This advert uses the Bango Txt Trigger Service to promote the site: more on this in Chapter 15.

Sending the message costs Mel £1.50 (it'll appear on her next phone bill). But our site hasn't made any money yet. Mel can use the money to buy content from our site or any other site that uses the Bango Service to charge for content. Only when she spends the money with us will we receive anything. In effect, Bango operates a "pay as you go" system: customers "top up" their Bango account with money they can then spend on content.

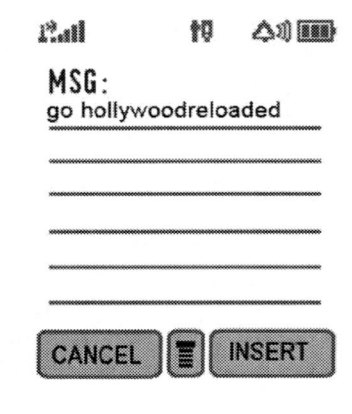

Notice that Mel hasn't had to sign up to anything: the Bango system has automatically created an account for her. It identified her as a new customer based on information sent along invisibly with the text message by the network provider or WAP gateway.

Mel will next receive a text message from Bango. The message tells her to either wait for a follow-up message that semi-automatically sends her to the Hollywood Reloaded site (a "WAP Push" message) or to start a WAP session herself and enter a particular URL. The experience here depends very much on Mel's phone. With some phones (such as the Sony Ericsson T68i) it's easier to simply select the URL in the first message to start a WAP session.

Whichever method Mel uses, she ends up at the Hollywood Reloaded home page with £1.50 to spend. She selects the Gossip link, and then the first item of gossip—the article we're charging for. This link goes to the URL http://bango.net/111234567910.

When she selects the link, the Bango system receives the request and recognises Mel from her unique identifier. Because the Bango Number being used in this link has a charge set against it, the Bango system now checks whether Mel can pay. In this case she can, as we're charging 20p for the link and she has £1.50 credit. If she didn't have enough credit, the Bango system would recommend a method of topping up her credit based on various criteria such as the country she's in and her network provider. The system supports payment methods including premium SMS messages, operator billing systems, debit/credit card payments, and PIN codes purchased using premium-rate voice phone calls (see Appendix 4 for full details).

As Mel has sufficient credit, Bango displays a page indicating the cost of the content and asks Mel to confirm that she wants to pay. If she agrees, Bango simply charges the cost of the page to her account and redirects her to the content. And we've made some money!

Mel can access the other content we're charging for in the same way. She doesn't need to top up her account until she tries to access something she doesn't have enough credit to pay for.

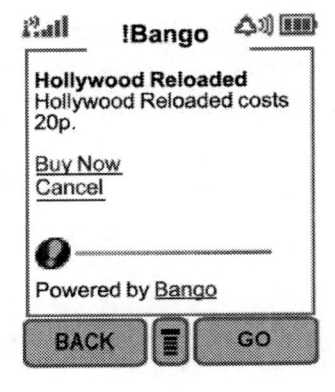

```
!Bango
Hollywood Reloaded
Hollywood Reloaded costs 20p.
Buy Now
Cancel

Powered by Bango
BACK        GO
```

It's important to understand that the £1.50 credit Mel started with is *not* associated with our site in any way. Mel can spend some of it on our site and some of it elsewhere.

## Checking revenue

Once you're making money you'll want to know how much! The Members' Lounge includes screens for checking current and past revenue, showing exactly how much money you're earning and how much you're growing. You can also use these screens to track usage for any of your Bango Numbers, including those associated with content that's free to access.

## Limitations

Although the Hollywood Reloaded site is a money-earner, there are some obvious—and not-so-obvious—limitations.

- **We can only charge for a few pieces of content.** That's because we bought the Focus package in our example. Buying a more expensive package would give us a few more Bango Numbers to use for charging, or we could buy additional Bango Numbers for our Focus package.

With much larger sites it becomes more effective to use the features of the Bango Relay Service, only available with the Pro, Focus and Express packages, which allows us to use one Bango Number to charge for access to more than one piece of content (see Chapter 9 for more details).

- **Customers can access the content when not authorised to do so**. We'll explain why this is so, and discuss what you can do about it, in Chapter 11.

- **The site's *static*: based on files that never change.** This means that if we want to change the site too dramatically—for example, add our logo on each content page—we need to change every page. It also makes it harder to add new content, since we need to change index pages, write content pages, and so on. And more worryingly it makes compatibility more difficult, since we have to manually keep our pages up-to-date as new phones appear or we convert content to support existing phones. To scale up—support more customers, more phones, more content—then a *dynamic* site would be better—see below.

## Creating a dynamic site

The solution to the scalability and flexibility problems of a static site like our example is to use a *dynamic* site. A dynamic site uses programming techniques to create WML (or HTML, or anything) as required and send it straight back to the phone (or web browser, and so on) without saving the result in a file. The programs are stored and run on the web server, not on the phone.

All high-traffic, high-content web sites use these dynamic techniques—whether on the mobile internet or the fixed internet. Popular programming languages involved are PHP (www.php.net), Perl (www.perl.org) and ASP (http://msdn.microsoft.com/asp/).

With all dynamic sites, part of the URL for a page within the site identifies the program that's to be run, and part of it identifies additional information the program needs to produce the most appropriate output—these are known as the *parameters*. The program examines and checks the parameters, takes any action needed to discover or produce the correct output for the phone, and then sends it back to the phone.

Dynamic sites let you determine what phone your customer is using and present only the content that's suitable for that phone. This even includes formatting that content (resizing images, for example) on demand.

To discover what phone's being used you check the HTTP_USER_AGENT variable available to your server-side program. Every phone model and version has its own value for HTTP_USER_AGENT. You can determine a phone's capabilities by looking up that value in the WURFL (see Appendix 1). Some phones also send through the URL for their UAProf file—another way to determine its capabilities—see Appendix 1.

With dynamic sites you can also dynamically generate index files by, for example, using queries against a database of your content. Well-designed dynamic sites make it much easier to add content to your site.

Many books and web sites help you learn how to create dynamic web sites: that extensive subject is outside the scope of this book. However, to use the Bango Relay Service (described in Chapter 9) or the Bango Identifier Service (described in Chapter 10) you need to understand and use dynamic web site techniques.

## Summary

In this chapter we've turned our simple free site into a money-earner by signing up for Bango services and making some straightforward changes. We've seen how easy it is for users to pay for our content, but we've learned that our simple site has limitations: it'll be hard to maintain as it grows, and there are ways that people can access the content when not authorised to do so.

But we've made a significant step. Our site can start to make money while we learn how to take it to the next level.

# Chapter 8
# Content ratings and access restrictions

Not all content on the mobile internet is suitable for everyone. Some content—adult or violent content—should have restricted access. This chapter is devoted to this important issue.

## Introduction

As with the fixed internet, all forms of adult entertainment and services are very popular on mobile devices. All types of adult entertainment are well represented in the mobile world, including:

- Gambling, lotteries and gaming
- Video games including violence and role-play involving drugs
- Sexually explicit images and videos
- Chat and dating services

If you plan to provide any services designed for adult entertainment, you must ensure that you are fully aware of the laws relating to your service in the countries where you intend to operate. For example, in some countries you may not be able to use location-based services unless users can verify they are over 18. Gambling may be illegal or subject to special rules about posting of bonds. Some erotic material may be deemed illegal in many countries.

Not only do you have to be aware of legal restrictions, you must also consider restrictions imposed by mobile operators who may want to act as "gatekeepers" to people using phones connected through their network.

As soon as your content is Bango-enabled it is accessible to more than 300 million users in dozens of countries through hundreds of mobile operators. It is also accessible to people of all ages and cultures, who you can collect money from for your service.

## Bango adult content policies

Because you're using the Bango system to sell your content, you need to be aware of Bango's policies in this area. Fortunately, Bango has laid out its policies very clearly. Bango does not supply content: it simply acts as a content discovery and payment infrastructure.

1. Bango respects and supports the right of individuals and organisations to protect children from access to inappropriate services.
2. Bango fully implements mobile operator content access guidelines.
3. Bango ensures content providers provide necessary and accurate information to enable implementation of the end-user and mobile operator obligations.
4. Bango will take a lead in working with other key industry players to implement and evolve its policies.
5. To provide tools to help content providers comply with relevant legislation that applies to them where their services are used.

# Bango services

Bango provides several services to help content providers act in a responsible way, to meet their obligations to deliver only legal content, and to help parents and guardians restrict access to inappropriate material.

- Content providers classify all sites they register with Bango as *U* (Universal) or *R* (Restricted), similar to ratings for cinema films.
- Content providers receive regular bulletins from Bango on changes in operator policies that Bango becomes aware of.

## Mobile operator rules and regulations

As well as allowing Bango to help ensure that people can restrict access to adult-only content, content ratings also help Bango correctly apply rules laid down by mobile operators.

Many mobile operators are implementing *filters* to prevent children accessing potentially harmful content. These filters can't inspect Java or BREW-based applications or video streams, so these must by default be blocked from all users except those verified as adult. However, in these situations, mobile operators may accept *whitelist* entries from Bango—effectively, lists of approved content—to bypass the filters. You'll need to submit your site for whitelisting to make sure it can still be accessed: you can do this using the Bango Members' Lounge.

In the UK, if you operate an R-rated site and want to use the Bango Txt Trigger Service to promote it, you must promote it with either a 69xxx or 89xxx short code—see the Members' Lounge for an up-to-date list of Bango short codes. Some operators may bar access to this short code where the sender can't be verified as being 18 or over. For U-rated content you must promote your site using the short code 83055. See Chapter 15 for more about this service.

Bango implements age verification on behalf of mobile operators for users whose age is unknown. For content providers using Bango services, variations in operator requirements are automatically supported.

## Rating guidelines

1. **Correctly classify your content.** To protect the integrity of the whitelist, sanctions may be applied to any content that is classified as U-rated but should be R-rated.

2. **Register the "top level" of any site containing *only* U-rated content in the Bango database.** It will then be automatically submitted to the whitelisting process. This is vital for videos and Java or BREW-based applications, which will otherwise be inaccessible.

3. **Keep U-rated and R-rated content separate.** This means keep them in parallel: never put R-rated content "inside" a U-rated site. Using separate sites ensures the R-rated content won't be whitelisted. You

can link between the two sites *but only if* the U-rated site links to the R-rated site through a Bango Number that's classified as R—a "beaded curtain".

Please note that the terms and conditions of your contract with Bango make clear that it's your responsibility to rate your content appropriately. Bango can't provide legal advice about content, as it does not have expertise in this area, and has no content itself.

## Rating your content

You use the Members' Lounge to rate your content at the same time you define the URL(s) that each of your Bango Numbers points to. Each Bango Number has its own rating, so you can mark some content as universal and some restricted if necessary. You can change the ratings for your Bango Numbers at any time.

To rate your content, first go to http://bango.com/members in your web browser and log in. Then go to the Manage Content section to see all the Bango Numbers in your Bango package (if you have more than one package click the appropriate Edit Numbers button to see its Bango Numbers). Finally click the Bango Number that corresponds to the URL you want to rate.

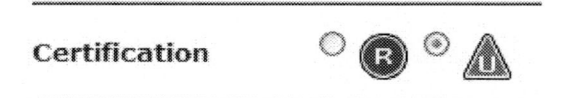

**Certification**     ○ ⓡ ⊙ ⚠

Select the appropriate certification, and then click Make Changes to confirm the certification.

Chapter 9
# The Bango Relay Service

In previous chapters all the Bango Numbers we've used have had one function: they've acted as a pointer to a URL, and might have had a fee associated with them to let you charge for access. The message has been: one Bango Number, one "thing".

Occasionally we've hinted at the mysterious Bango Relay Service, suggesting it can help you solve problems with security, scalability and flexibility. We'll explore this service in this chapter and show you how.

To make use of the Bango Relay Service you'll need to understand and use dynamic techniques within your mobile internet site—see Chapter 7.

## What is the Bango Relay Service?

The goal of the Bango Relay Service is to help you provide a better service to your customers, and so grow your revenue.

The Bango Relay Service provides additional functionality to Bango Numbers. A Bango Number endowed with Relay functionality (often called a *Bango Relay Number*) can be used within your site in more ways than a number without that functionality. As well as the existing (and lucrative!) charge-then-redirect service, the key additional features when using Bango Relay Numbers are:

- **Information passing.** You can pass almost any information from your site through the Bango system and out the other end to your destination URL.
- **User IDs.** You can uniquely identify the customer who bought your content.
- **Security tokens.** You can ensure nobody can access your content without being charged.

- **Dynamic pricing.** You can set the price of an item of content within your site, and the Bango system will honour that price.

The Bango Relay Service is only available to subscribers of the Pro, Focus, and Express packages. It's not available to Micro package subscribers.

## Historical note

The Bango system previously used a special number format to identify the Bango Numbers with Relay functionality. These old-style Bango Relay Numbers, which were then called "Fingerprint Numbers", were always ten digits long and began 0000.

This has now changed: any Bango Number can be given Relay functionality.

# Benefits of the Bango Relay Service

- **Your costs don't increase as your site grows.** The information-passing ability means you don't need one Bango Number for each piece of content you want to charge for. You can pass information about the content through the Bango system, and it will be included within the destination URL where you can ensure you deliver the appropriate content to the customer.

- **You can ensure customers pay the charges you set.** The security tokens are unique transaction IDs passed to a Bango Number's destination URL. If you see the same token more than once, someone's trying to cheat the system and you can ensure they don't receive any content. You can also detect price-fixing by checking that the price paid is the price you expected to be paid.

- **You can use transaction logs to recommend content and target high-spending customers.** You can log the user ID and content sold for each transaction, and mine that valuable data in any way you want. You can't find out names, addresses or phone numbers but you can identify, for example, that a number of people all bought the same range of content—and then recommend additional content to a customer on that basis.

# Bango Relay Service inputs and outputs

With the Bango Relay Service we begin to see the Bango system as having both inputs and outputs. We're used to supplying inputs—the Bango Numbers—as a part of the URLs that cause customers to be charged. The Bango system redirects customers to our URL, but until now hasn't supplied us with any additional information. That now changes.

Here's what the new system looks like:

- Input parameters are the Bango Number (required), any custom parameters you want to be preserved (optional), the price you want to charge (optional, defaulting to the price set for the Bango Number in the Bango system), the number of accesses allowed (optional, if configured for a maximum number of accesses), the length of time for which access is allowed (optional, if configured for timed access), a page title (optional—Pro package only) and content title (optional—Pro package only).
- Output parameters are the Bango Number passed as input, the custom parameters (if supplied as input), the customer's unique user ID, the transaction's security token and the price charged to the customer.

With the Bango Relay Service both input and output parameters are specified as part of the URL.

An *input URL*—a Bango URL you place on your site to charge a customer—might look like this:

`http://bango.net/go.aspx?bango=111234567910&p=epzero`

This is slightly different to the style of URL we've used in previous chapters. Here the Bango Number is passed as the value of the parameter `bango`, and we've added our own custom information, `epzero`, as the value of the `p` parameter. See below for more on this.

An *output URL*—a URL that Bango sends back to your customer after charging them, which redirects to your site—might look like this:

`http://wap.example.com/deliverContent.php?b=11123456791`
`0&p=epzero&u=1234567&t=07BF24EC5A1B98FF5CDB4379EAABC310`
`&c=20`

The first part—up to but not including the ?—is the destination URL specified in the Manage Content section for this Bango Number. The rest is added by the Bango Relay Service. You'll see it preserved our Bango Number in the b parameter and our custom information in the p parameter. There are more parameters too: the u parameter is the unique customer ID; the scary-looking t parameter is the unique transaction ID; and the c parameter is the price paid by the customer within that transaction.

The program `deliverContent.php` running on the content provider's site would then use the parameters supplied to do whatever it's designed to do—which would hopefully include delivering the content the customer has paid for!

In the following sections we'll examine each input and output parameter in turn, and what you can do with them.

## Information passing with the p parameter

Any information you pass to the Bango Relay Service with the p parameter will be preserved and appear unchanged within the p parameter passed to the destination URL for that Bango Number.

You can use this parameter for anything you want. Some examples:

- **An identifier for the content being purchased.** This is how you can use just one Bango Number to charge for your entire collection of content. You pass an identifier for the content within the p parameter of the input URL, and it'll appear within the p parameter of the output URL. Your content identifier can be a word, a number, or whatever you decide to use to uniquely identify the content on your site.

- **A session ID.** You may want to track the path someone takes within your site using a random session ID. Encoding this within the p parameter ensures it's preserved across a Bango transaction.

You must *URL encode* the information you're passing in the input URL, and *URL decode* it again from the output URL. This encoding/decoding sequence ensures that URLs are properly formed and don't contain illegal characters. URL encoding is defined in internet RFC 1738 (http://www.faqs.org/rfcs/rfc1738.html).

You can only use one p parameter within each input URL. However, if you want to send more than one piece of information you can: just combine the information however you want, and make sure it's properly encoded and decoded. For example, you might want to pass both a content ID and a session ID. We could combine them as the single string `c=epzero&s=12341234` and then URL encode that to make `c%3Depzero%26s%3D12341234`—which can be supplied as the value of the p parameter in our input URL. Of course we'd need to URL decode that string at the other end of the process and then split the two parameters before we could make use of them.

## Detecting your customers using the u parameter

First the bad news: you can't determine your customers' names, addresses or phone numbers from the information that Bango supplies you with. You can, however, distinguish between each customer—and combine this knowledge with the other information supplied in the output URL in any way you want.

Bango identifies each customer from information sent through from the gateways and mobile network operators. When someone first accesses the Bango Service they're given a unique numerical ID within the Bango system—not related to the gateway or operator identifier.

This user ID is included in the output URL as the value of the u parameter. It tells you which customer purchased the content.

Some example uses for this information:

- You can keep track of repeat purchases. Are the same customers returning again and again to buy more content, or are most of your sales one-offs?
- You can personalise the site for your customers. For example, you can list the content they've already bought (see also Chapter 10).
- You can recommend additional content: "customers who bought this also bought..."
- You can reply to customer queries about their purchase history.

# Increasing security using the t parameter

The Bango Relay Service's security tokens are unique transaction IDs. They certify that a customer has gone through the Bango system and paid to access the content. A token is never issued more than once by the Bango system. You can use this information to ensure that only paying customers are accessing your content.

A security token is included in an output URL as the value of the t parameter. An example token is:

07BF24EC5A1B98FF5CDB4379EAABC310

Tokens are always hexadecimal (base 16) numbers of 32 digits—in other words, only numbers 0-9 and letters A-F. Bango always uses upper case letters in security tokens.

We'll show how you can use security tokens to protect your valuable content in Chapter 11.

# Dynamic pricing with the c parameter

With the Bango Relay Service you can dynamically set the price for any piece of content, based on any criteria you choose. Some benefits of this:

- You can charge different prices using just one Bango Relay Number.
- Each piece of content can have a different price.
- You can set a price of 1 to test the service without changing the price for users.
- You can give a customer access to content at a reduced price or at no price if they're having trouble downloading the content.

The c parameter is also used within an output URL as described below.

## Within the input URL

You set the price for a piece of content by including the c parameter within an input URL. This parameter overrides the default price set for the Bango Number in the Manage Content section.

There are limitations: you can't change the currency (it's always the same as the currency used in the Manage Content section) or the charging method (single, multiple or timed access—see Chapter 18). You're also limited to a number between 0 and 600—any price up to £6, €6 or $6. Any attempt to use a price outside this range will cause the customer to be charged the default price.

## Within the output URL

The c parameter is always included as part of the output URL. Its meaning depends on the charging method in use for the content, as defined in the Manage Content section for this Bango Number (see Chapter 18).

- **Single access.** Here the value of the c parameter records precisely how much the customer was charged for the content.
- **Multiple or timed access.** Here the c parameter will record the price charged, but only for the first visit. Subsequent visits up to the limit defined for this Bango Number will be recorded by setting the value of the c parameter in the output URL to -2.

Also, if the price in the input URL was set to a number outside the range of 0-600, the value of the c parameter in the output URL will be -1.

## Detecting price-fixing

As the price can be set in the input URL, there's nothing to stop a malicious user from forming their own input URL and setting the price to anything they like.

The Bango system will honour whatever is set for the c parameter in the input URL, and preserves that value in the output URL. This means you can check the price actually charged against the price you intended to charge—before you deliver the content.

For example, if a malicious user sets c=1, they'll be charged 1p (or 1c) for the content and c=1 will appear in the output URL processed by the content provider. If the content provider's records indicate the price for that content should be 100, a simple comparison can detect the attempted price-fix and return an error page rather than the content.

Note that in this scenario the malicious user has paid 1p and received nothing—so not only has the content provider lost nothing, he's gained revenue!

# Changing access limits using the na and ta parameters

If a Bango Number is configured to charge a particular amount for multiple accesses (rather than for a single access), you can change the number of accesses allowed by passing the na parameter in the input URL. For example, passing na=10 limits the customer to ten accesses.

Similarly, you can use the ta parameter to change the time for which a customer may access the content, if the Bango Number is configured for timed access. The units (minutes, hours or days) can't be changed in this way, and the value of the ta parameter always uses the units configured in the Manage Content section. For example, pass ta=20 to allow a customer access for 20 minutes (or hours or days, depending on the Bango Number's configured units).

You can use these parameters in conjunction with the c parameter to change both the price charged and the access limits for the content at the time of purchase.

# Page and content titles using the pt and ct parameters

The Bango Relay Service is ideal for charging for multiple items of content. But unless you tell it, the service can't explain to your customers exactly what they're paying for.

Normally the payment page—the page inserted by Bango before customers reach the content—describes what the customer is buying using the title defined for the Bango Number in the Manage Content section. You can override this title, and include an additional title for the content being purchased, using the pt and ct parameters in the input URL. (Note that you can only use these parameters if you subscribe to the Pro package.)

The values for both these parameters are URL-encoded strings. For example, to set the page title to "Hollywood Gossip" and the content title to "Episode Zero" you would include the following within the input URL:

pt=Hollywood%20Gossip&ct=Episode%20Zero

If you set the title in the Manage Content section appropriately you shouldn't need to use the pt parameter. However, we recommend using the ct parameter wherever you can for the best customer experience.

# Assigning Bango Relay functionality to a Bango Number

The Bango package you subscribe to determines how many of your Bango Numbers are eligible for Bango Relay functionality. You can also buy the right to give that functionality to more Bango Numbers.

To assign Bango Relay functionality to a number, first go to http://bango.com/members in your web browser and log in. Then go to the Manage Content section to see all the Bango Numbers in your Bango package (if you have more than one package click the appropriate Edit Numbers button to see its Bango Numbers).

On the left, click the Bango Number you want to have Bango Relay functionality. You'll see all the details of the number, such as the destination URLs defined for each supported device type. Within the Relay section, click Assign.

You can use the Advanced page of the Manage Content section to manage Bango Relay functionality for your Bango Numbers, and to buy the right to assign that functionality to more of your Bango Numbers.

# Improvements to the Bango Relay Service

Bango occasionally adds new functionality to the Bango Relay Service. In some cases this functionality may be restricted to customers who subscribe to the Pro package.

For full details of any additional Bango Relay functionality, check the Members' Lounge for updated documentation.

Chapter 10
# The Bango Identifier Service

We've seen in the previous chapter that Bango identifies each customer uniquely with a user ID, and the Bango Relay Service tells you a user's unique ID when they purchase content. But what if you just want to identify the user without charging them? Identifying users early would allow you to enhance the user experience and personalise it—presenting content you know a customer will want to buy, displaying a list of previous purchases, and so on.

The Bango Identifier Service lets you do this. It works in a similar way to the Bango Relay Service, but never charges the user. We'll explain the inputs and outputs of this service in this chapter.

The Bango Identifier Service is only available to subscribers of the Focus and Pro packages. It's not available to Express or Micro package subscribers.

## Bango Identifier Service inputs and outputs

As with the Bango Relay Service, it's best to think of the Bango Identifier Service as having inputs and outputs. You provide the service with certain inputs, and it responds with certain outputs that include information you need to uniquely identify a user—and be able to trust that identity.

Here are the inputs and outputs of the Bango Identifier Service:

- Input parameters are the Bango Number (required), any custom parameters you want to be preserved (optional), and whether you want a user to manually log in if the system can't identify them any other way (optional).

- Output parameters are the Bango Number passed as input, the custom parameters (if supplied as input), the customer's unique user ID, an indicator of whether that user is barred from accessing R-rated content, and an indicator that this user has been identified using the Bango Identifier Service.

With the Bango Identifier Service both input and output parameters are specified as part of the URL.

An *input URL*—a Bango URL you place on your site to identify a customer—might look like this:

`http://bango.net/id.aspx?bango=123456&p=anydata&login=n`

This is similar to the Bango Relay Service URL: but note that it uses `id.aspx` not `go.aspx`.

An *output URL*—a URL that Bango sends back to your customer after identifying them, which redirects to your site—might look like this:

`http://wap.example.com/personalise.php?bango=123456&p=anydata&u=9876543&a=0&id=y&t=1BF5CDB4379EA98F4EC5AABC31007BF2&`

The first part—up to but not including the ?—is the destination URL specified in the Manage Content section for this Bango Number. The rest is added by the Bango Identifier Service. The original Bango Number is included, as is the data we passed in the p parameter. You'll be familiar with the u and t parameters from the Bango Relay Service. The a parameter tells you whether the user's barred from accessing R-rated content, and the id parameter indicates that the user has been identified using the Bango Identifier Service.

The program `personalise.php` running on the content provider's site would then use the parameters supplied to present a personalised experience to the identified user.

In the following sections we'll examine each input and output parameter in turn, and what you can do with them.

## Information passing with the p parameter

As with the Bango Relay Service, you can use this parameter to pass any information you want through to the output URL. You can include as many pieces of information you want, encoded within the same p parameter. Don't forget to URL encode and decode the information at each end!

For more information about this parameter, see the appropriate section in Chapter 9.

## Manual login and the login parameter

In most cases Bango can identify users from information supplied automatically by gateways and mobile network operators. In some cases, however, this isn't possible: these users must identify themselves manually by supplying their phone number and a password.

When producing a personalised site using the Bango Identifier Service you may feel that you don't want to force users to log in if the Bango system can't identify them automatically. You could then present these users with a slightly different page.

By default the Bango Identifier Service will ask users to manually log in if they're not automatically identified. To stop this process happening, pass `login=n` as part of the input URL.

(Leaving out the `login` parameter is equivalent to using `login=y`.)

If you choose not to force manual login, then you must deal with cases where the user is not identified. In these cases, the output URL's u parameter is always 0.

## Identifying your customers using the u parameter

As with the Bango Relay Service, the u parameter in the output URL is the user's unique identifier in the Bango system. You can use this identifer with other information in your own systems to present personalised content to the user.

The Bango Relay Service and Bango Identifier Service will always return the same identifier for the same user.

## Trusting identity using the t parameter

The Bango Identifier Service's security tokens are unique IDs. They certify that a customer has gone through the Bango system and has been successfully identified. In effect, they give you the ability to trust the identification details supplied.

A security token is included in an output URL as the value of the t parameter. An example token is:

1BF5CDB4379EA98F4EC5AABC31007BF2

Tokens are always hexadecimal (base 16) numbers of 32 digits—in other words, only numbers 0-9 and letters A-F. Bango always uses upper case letters in security tokens.

We'll show how you can validate a token—and so trust an identity—in Chapter 11.

## Checking barring status with the a parameter

Any user on the Bango system may be barred from accessing R-rated content (see Chapter 8). Information about a given user's barring status is returned as part of the output URL, in the a parameter.

If a user is barred from accessing R-rated content, then a will be set to 1 (the output URL will include a=1).

If a user is not barred, then a will be set to 0 (the output URL will include a=0).

If a user is not identified in the output URL (u=0), the a parameter is not supplied.

You must make sure that barred users only have access to U-rated content.

## Confirming identification with the id parameter

A particular Bango Number can be assigned both Identifier functionality and Relay functionality—you can use it both to identify users and to charge them for access to content. This lets you use the same destination URL (defined in the Manage Content section for the Bango Number) to handle both cases, if you need to.

To allow this URL to distinguish between Relay and Identifier usage—and to then either present the purchased content or to personalise a page—the Bango Identifier Service's output URL always includes id=y.

If the id parameter is not set, the Bango Identifier Service was not used.

Note that the Bango Identifier Service never charges a user even if a charge is set against the associated Bango Number.

## Assigning Bango Identifier functionality to a Bango Number

The Bango package you subscribe to determines how many of your Bango Numbers are eligible for Bango Identifier functionality. You can also buy the right to give that functionality to more Bango Numbers.

To assign Bango Identifier functionality to a number, first go to http://bango.com/members in your web browser and log in. Then in the Manage Content section, click Advanced for your package, and then click Manage Identifiers. This page lets you assign Bango Identifier functionality to your Bango Numbers, and to buy the right to assign that functionality to more of your Bango Numbers.

Note that Bango Numbers assigned with Bango Identifier functionality must be U-rated to ensure that the Bango Identifier Service can identify users who are barred from R-rated content.

# Chapter 11
# Security and digital rights management

Your content is your livelihood. You want to be sure that only those who pay can access your content, and that they can only access it for as long as they're authorised.

In this chapter we'll discuss how to stop unauthorised use of your valuable content, including how you can use Bango's digital rights management technologies to help.

## Digital rights management

*Digital rights management* is the name given to all issues involving the control of access to digital data. For example, Apple's near-ubiquitous iPod portable music player uses digital rights management to control what you can do with music you buy from the iTunes Music Store.

When most people talk about digital rights management, they talk about technology. But underlying this broad topic are the basic, well-established legal frameworks of copyright law. Digital rights management attempts to enforce copyright restrictions using technology—to stop people performing "unauthorised acts" on the copyrighted material, such as copying it. Without this layer of technology, though, copyright still holds: a copyright infringement is a copyright infringement whether technology is involved or not (and whether the person infringing knows it's an infringement or not).

We can't give legal advice—please contact your legal advisor—but broadly, anything expressed in "tangible form" is copyrighted, automatically. This means that any image you create, any text you write, any video you direct, and any game you develop, are your copyright. This gives *you* the right to decide what others are permitted to do with that content. (Of course, there's a lot more to this important topic that we can't cover here. We recommend you spend time researching this area, and talk to your legal advisor.)

Once you add your content to your mobile internet site, it can be very hard to enforce your copyright. The digital rights management technologies available from Bango can help. It's important to understand, though, that *no security system is perfect*. A security fence is as strong as the weakest link: and no good at all if the gates are wide open. Think carefully about how you protect your content, and remember that security is a *process*, not a *product*.

## Unauthorised access

In Chapter 7 we described some limitations of the example "Hollywood Reloaded" site, including the ability for customers to access the content when not authorised to do so. What do we mean by this?

Remember how the charging system works. In place of a link to the content, you include a link to the Bango site, referencing the Bango Number. The Bango system extracts the appropriate payment, and then redirects the customer to the URL associated with the Bango Number.

As far as you're concerned, the only authorised access is using the Bango Number: any other access is unauthorised. There are, however, two ways to access the content without using the Bango Number.

### Bookmarking after payment

After authorised access to the content—after they've gone through the Bango system, and paid for access—a customer can bookmark the content page on their mobile browser.

You might not consider this an important problem: the customer has paid for the content, so you might not care if they visit the content again without paying once more. But you might feel this unauthorised access is unfairly reducing your profits.

It also raises an important consideration: you need to be very careful when choosing which pages to charge for. Don't charge for access to a page where the content changes—for example, an index page.

Let's imagine you create an index page for all your chargeable content, and—to make best use of your scarce Bango Numbers—you set a charge against that index page rather than the content itself. This would mean your customers could bookmark the index page after paying once, and never have to pay again to visit that page—or any of the content to which it links, which you might change over time.

To preserve your revenue, charge for each piece of content, not index pages. This helps to minimise the problem with bookmarks.

### Direct URL

The Bango system is a charge-and-redirect service. If someone discovers the URL that the Bango system redirects to, they can bypass the system and access the content for free.

To exploit this problem someone would need to know or guess the URL for your content. In our Hollywood Reloaded example, we use numbers in the filenames for pieces of content—not hard to guess once you've seen some free content—but we also add a short description, which would be less easy to guess.

We could increase the difficulty by adding random junk to the filenames. We should also make sure that our web server is configured to disallow directory listings—to stop our attempted freeloader from going to http://examples.bango.net/hollywoodreloaded/content/ and discovering our filenames that way.

However we try to hide our chargeable content, we're still practising "security by obscurity"—relying on people not discovering our URLs to preserve our revenue. This is not a good idea.

## Protecting your content

To prevent unauthorised access using the bookmarking or direct-URL methods, you need to write additional code. A simple method is available from the Bango Members' Lounge.

For better security the Bango Relay Service (Chapter 9) and the Bango Identifier Service (Chapter 10) offer *security tokens* to let you validate transactions and trust identities. These security tokens are unique IDs, never issued more than once, which certify that a customer has gone through the Bango system. Each security token is a 32-character hexadecimal string, included in the output URL of the Bango system for both services as the value of the t parameter.

You use the fact that the Bango system never issues the same token twice to ensure that only authorised customers are accessing your content. Put simply, if you see a token twice you know the second access using that token is unauthorised.

If Bango doesn't issue a token twice, how might one be seen more than once by your site? There are a few plausible reasons, including:

- A paying customer might have innocently bookmarked a content page after purchase, and returned to it from the bookmark. (The bookmarked URL will include the security token.) This isn't necessarily an attempt to cheat payment, just an honest mistake.
- The token might have been "sniffed" in transit across the network—what's called a *man-in-the-middle attack*—by someone trying to avoid payment.

There are two ways you can use security tokens to protect your valuable content and trust the information supplied.

## Standard security checking

If you see a token more than once, you know that the second appearance is fake: it hasn't been issued by the Bango system. This means a simple but non-scalable security check is to keep a record of each token you receive from the Bango system.

Each time you process a request to your output URL you first extract the security token from the URL and search for it within your stored list of tokens. If there's no match, success! You add the new token to the list and proceed to the next step (supply the customer with the content or a personalised page as appropriate). If you've seen the token before then you display an error page.

This check doesn't detect an attacker who guesses a valid token that hasn't previously been issued.

## Advanced security checking

Bango keeps records of every user transaction or request to identify a user, including the generated security token and the ID of the user. Your site can query the Bango system remotely to validate a token.

To do this, you send an HTTP request within your code to the Bango token verifier URL, supplying the security token and the user ID you received in the output URL. The verifier URL has the form:

```
http://xml.bango.net/tokencheck.asp?t=token&u=user
```

The Bango system will respond with either of the following XML documents:

```
<?xml version="1.0"?>
<response success="true">
</response>
```

or

```
<?xml version="1.0"?>
<response success="false">
</response>
```

Bango expects to extend this XML response in the future.

Some important things to note about this check:

- You can only check a token/user ID combination once. When a "true" response is returned by the system the token is automatically expired: any further checks for that token and user ID will return a "false" response.
- Security tokens automatically expire five minutes after being generated. If you try to validate a token more than five minutes after it's generated you'll receive a "false" response.

This advanced check will defend against attackers who reverse-engineer the security token format (or who read this book!). However, it does introduce some latency: you can't deliver the content to the customer until you've asked Bango to validate the token and received a response.

## Summary

Using Bango's digital rights management technology to protect your valuable content can help preserve your revenue and avoid unauthorised access by attackers trying to infringe your copyright. But security is a process, not a product. Securing your content requires careful thought and planning, and a recognition that any security system is only as strong as the weakest link.

Part III
# Attracting customers to your site—and keeping them

In this part of the book we'll show you how to bring paying customers to your mobile internet site, and make them return again and again.

We'll give you tips on choosing the best Bango Number for your business. We'll cover the promotional tools at your disposal. And we'll talk about revenue, including tips on setting your content charges and information on dealing with Bango.

This part of the book is primarily aimed at a non-technical audience. Read this if you're **promoting** the mobile internet site.

## Chapter 12
# The three Cs: customers, content, chutzpah

Mobile internet sites aren't sprinkled with magic pixie dust to make them immune from the real world. So let's start this part of the book with the basics: the things every good business needs to understand. Knowing what follows can't guarantee success—but not knowing them almost guarantees failure.

## Customers, customers, customers

It may be obvious, but it bears repeating: your customers pay your salary.

What does this mean? Keep your customers happy. Service with a smile. The customer is always right. Well, maybe not all the time: but to paraphrase Bill Clinton, "It's the customers, stupid".

### Who are your customers?

Many businesses fail at this first hurdle. To sell, you need to define who you want to sell to. More than that: you should know every intimate detail of their lives. Your target market should be tattooed on the inside of your eyelids.

Let's use the example of a ringtones business. It's easy, right? Top ten tunes, top ten ringtones? Maybe. But seemingly everyone's in the business of selling today's hits as ringtones. Could you make money from a market as crowded as that one? Well, some people are, so maybe you could too. But markets are skewed towards the existing players: it's very hard to break into a mature market.

So what do you do? You think more carefully about who you want to sell to. The teenage market is saturated, you might say, so you don't want to sell to them. What about twentysomethings or thirtysomethings? They're just as likely to have mobiles as teenagers. But do they buy ringtones? And if so, what ringtones do they buy?

Know your customers. If your research on thirtysomethings tells you they're listening more and more to what they used to call "old people's radio" but which now seems strangely seductive, then what are those radio stations playing? You might find a market there. Or you might not.

This book can't tell you *who* to sell to, or what to sell them. That's for you to discover. If you find a niche, or open up a new market, then exploit it: you may become the dominant player, leaving everyone else trailing in your wake.

Once your business is up and running you can see whether you *really* know your customers by keeping track of your site statistics, and verifying that site changes you make result in greater earnings. See Chapter 19 for more on tracking site usage.

## Customer care

When dealing with a customer, imagine yourself in their position. How would *you* like to be treated? Follow this approach and you generally can't go wrong. Be calm, be courteous, be considerate.

By far the majority of customers are reasonable. They'll politely explain their problem, and there'll be a simple solution that leaves both you and the customer happy (and hopefully the customer will return). But what happens if a customer's angry, or won't accept your answer? There are no easy solutions: just apply common sense, and liberal helpings of patience. And whatever you do, don't get angry yourself.

Here are a few things to remember when contacting a customer:

- **Be clear and concise—and grammatical!** Use simple phrases, and no overlong, complex sentences. Complexity is the enemy of understanding. To put it another way: if your customers don't understand what you say, they won't know what you mean.
- **Be professional.** Paying customers expect and deserve a professional service. Here's a trick: if you remember the customer's name, they'll

remember you. If you remember the name of the customer's wife/husband/partner/child/pet, they'll love you forever.

- **Don't get technical.** Jargon and technobabble are confusing and unintelligible to most people. All your customers care about is that they receive the service they've paid for.

- **If there's been a problem, apologise.** The simple act of saying sorry goes a long way towards satisfying the customer, even if it doesn't actually help solve the problem. Free stuff also helps!

- **Email can easily be misinterpreted.** The absence of body language or verbal cues can turn a simple problem into a confrontation. Some people use—and overuse—smileys (sometimes called "emoticons") like :-) to make it clear they're not being serious. But be careful: many people think they're unprofessional in customer communication. It's probably fair to assume that the younger the customer, the more they'd accept smileys in email. Alternatively, speaking to the customer directly—on the phone, or face-to-face—may be a better solution as it bypasses the possibility of misinterpretation by email.

You may find it useful to have a published complaints procedure. This helps to reassure your customers that you'll deal with them fairly and quickly, and you'll find it easier to handle "difficult" customers with the procedure to back you up. Customers hate being left in the dark: your procedure must state clearly how quickly you'll respond. A couple of days is OK; a couple of weeks is not. And you must respond!

## Gathering customer feedback

Customers are an excellent source for feedback, both good and bad. They'll tell you what's wrong, and if you're very lucky, they'll give you information that you can use to improve your service and make more money. Think about the best way to help your customers tell you what they think.

- **You could give out a phone number.** Most businesses have contact numbers to let people get in touch. If you do this, consider how you want to deal with "out-of-hours" calls. Also, do you want to let people text you their feedback?

- **You could use an email address.** Think about your typical customer: are they likely to have access to email? Some phones can send email, but not all. If you do this, consider setting up a special email address that's only used for customer feedback. This helps the feedback go to the right place, and also means you won't get additional unsolicited email ("spam") in your personal inbox.

- **You could include a feedback page on your site.** This requires extra code that your web site hosting provider might not allow. Some providers may include this code as part of your hosting package: check with them.

Whichever method you choose, don't expect a flood of feedback. Assume you'll get no feedback whatsoever, and be pleasantly surprised when you receive some.

If you're desperate for feedback, consider introducing a "feedback of the month" prize. The winner could receive some branded goodies, like a mug or baseball cap, or simply some free content.

Nobody likes better than to hear how wonderful they are, so follow up on the most useful feedback. Tell the customer how much you appreciated their comments. If their feedback leads you directly to change your service in some way—add a feature they suggested, for example—then give them a reward. That way, they might send you more ideas in the future. (The opposite approach—take someone's idea, implement it, and don't even say thanks—is virtually guaranteed to lose you customers, and give you a bad name.)

## Interpreting feedback

Some feedback is easy to interpret: a broken link, some wallpaper not downloading, or a problem with charging, for example. But often feedback is vague and generic. Interpreting this feedback requires patience, some gut feel, and an awareness of the "big picture": the context, rather than the detail, of the feedback.

It's important not to be defensive about feedback. Your customers are far more likely to send you negative feedback than positive feedback—it's human nature. People don't usually send feedback when something works, because they *expect* it to work.

If you receive negative feedback, take a deep breath. Let your mind mull over it. Don't shoot off a combative email in response, no matter how wrong you think the feedback is. Tell yourself how lucky you are that someone cares enough about the service you're providing to tell you how you can improve it—or even just that it needs improving. All feedback is valuable, even—some would say *especially*—if it disagrees with you.

If you receive positive feedback, relax in the glow. But don't think that this customer has uttered a universal truth: you might find that the next feedback you receive takes entirely the opposite viewpoint. Positive feedback is good to receive, and raises the spirits more than you'd think it would. If multiple people are working on your site, spread the word.

The key to interpreting feedback is to consider the feedback as a whole, not as a collection of individual items that each needs addressing. If one or two people tell you something, it's useful to know. If twenty or thirty do, it's something to address.

And above all: it's your service. You're the boss. If your gut tells you the feedback's wrong, and that your "Top 100 Staplers" wallpaper collection really *is* the Next Big Thing, nobody can stop you.

## Content, content, content

Your content makes you money: the best customer service in the world can't help if you don't have anything to sell. But is that it? Do you just upload some content, sit back and count the cash? Sadly it's not quite as easy as that. Just as in the section above, put yourself in your customer's position, and see what happens.

### What are you selling?

Earlier in this chapter we emphasised the importance of knowing your customer. Once you know your customer, you can figure out what they'll buy, and then you can sell it to them. It sounds so simple!

And, truth be told, it is, if you really know your customer. You'll know what they like, and what they dislike. You'll know not to sell them Java or BREW-based games if they don't typically have suitablly equipped phones (or don't typically play games). You'll watch the skies looking for any approaching (or receding) trends that you know they'll be influenced by.

Try not to restrict yourself to just one type of content. Although you might start small, leave room for growth and diversification. Concentrating on one type of content might work in the short term, but as trends come and go you might find your revenue stream drying up in the longer term. This can happen even if you created and dominate that market: the early bird catches the worm, but the quick brown fox jumps over the lazy dog.

## Refreshing your content

Most businesses find that a large proportion of their revenue comes from their existing, happy customers. What does this tell us?

- Keep your customers happy. We know that already, but it's always good to remind yourself.

- Human nature is to stick with what you know. Customers much prefer returning to a service they know and trust—one which delivers the goods—than to change.

- You can reinforce human nature by giving customers a reason to return: new content.

You may see existing customers returning even if you haven't changed your site in weeks. But they're not buying any more. Why have they returned? Because they want to buy from you again. What type of business turns away customers like that?

You can retain (and grow) your existing, happy, habitual customer base by regularly refreshing your content. Your dream scenario is a virtuous circle: regular returning customers as well as new customers. The new customers turn into existing customers, and the cycle repeats. (Some customers won't return. This customer "churn" is unavoidable, but you can help to keep it as low as possible by providing new, high-quality content.)

You don't need to replace your entire content on a weekly schedule, as the existing content could be attractive to new customers. A good strategy is to use a "rolling refresh", with new content clearly labelled (with the date it was added, for example) and older content moving out of the spotlight but still accessible.

Even a relatively small fraction of new content per week (or per month) can retain your loyal customers, and keep your revenue rising. In contrast, nothing reduces income more quickly than stale content.

For great content ideas and examples of what works, visit www.bango.com.

## Chutzpah, chutzpah, chutzpah

Have you ever had a conversation with someone and found yourself thinking, "The nerve of that guy"? That's chutzpah. A passionate belief in yourself, self-confidence, and more than a hint of arrogance or obnoxiousness.

You don't need to be obnoxious to build a profitable business from the mobile internet, but you do need the right mental approach: boldness, directness and a go-get-em attitude. You need to think positive, promote yourself and expect success. It also helps if you're willing to take a few risks here and there.

### Don't ask, don't get

Don't be afraid to ask favours. For example, if you find another mobile internet site aimed at a similar audience to yours (and you have no particular wish to compete with them), suggest some mutual back-scratching: you'll promote their site if they promote yours. They might say yes. (They might also say no, and start to think of you as a competitor. Consider whether the potential reward is worth the risk.)

### Self-promotion

You want to promote your brand and your products. One way to do that is to promote yourself. Name some well-known business leaders: chances are you'll think of global names like Rupert Murdoch or Bill Gates. But you might also know who runs a local business, or a small web site. You know the names of all these people because they're as adept at self-promotion as they are at business promotion. And they realise that by promoting themselves, they promote their businesses.

## No such thing as bad publicity?

Some businesses believe that any publicity is better than no publicity. They prefer, almost appear to relish, notoriety and infamy to more traditional press releases and adverts. It can sometimes work: I'm sure you can think of examples (the publicity worked!). But it's a dangerous tactic, which can backfire by alienating the very people you're trying to sell to. For a business just starting up, it's not worth the risk.

## Guerrilla marketing

Guerrilla marketing is a way to use scarce resources to maximum effect, usually by adopting an unconventional approach. It occasionally ties in with the previous section: you can buy notoriety much more cheaply than any other kind of publicity.

Guerrilla marketing isn't making sure your web site is listed properly in search engines. Guerrilla marketing is writing anonymous high-praise reviews of your web site on discussion boards. Or projecting your URL onto the side of a building. Or a thousand other on-the-edge ideas. We can't condone law-breaking, of course, but you don't have to break the law to promote your business in an imaginative way. Why not try brainstorming with friends over a drink or two?

# Chapter 13
# Choosing a Bango Number you can promote

To recap from Chapter 7, Bango sells a number of packages. Each package is bundled with different features, and includes the ability to reserve some *Bango Numbers* for use with your mobile shop. Bango Numbers are alternatives to URLs: you set up the Bango system to associate your Bango Number with your site (or a part of it) and set any charges for access.

A Bango Number can be used in two ways:

- As an *access number*—a route into your mobile internet site. This is a Bango Number you promote. In the Members' Lounge, you associate that number with the URL of your mobile internet site (or any other URL you like).

- As an *internal number* that your customers never need to see or use. These typically identify content you want to charge for, or are used for tracking accesses. They're Bango Numbers the techies need to care about.

There's no magic difference between access Bango Numbers and internal Bango Numbers: you can use any number for either purpose. But some numbers—the shorter ones—make better access numbers than internal numbers.

In this chapter we'll talk more about access numbers, how they fit into Bango packages, and how to choose the best ones for your business.

# Standard, Bronze, Silver and Gold numbers

The shorter the Bango Number, the better it is as an access number, the easier it is for customers to get to your site, and consequently the more valuable it is. Bango groups numbers into easy-to-understand categories:

- Standard numbers are 10-50 digits in length. Typically used as an internal billing number but can still be used as an access number.
- Bronze numbers have 8-9 digits. That sounds long, but full phone numbers are just as long, and when combined with phone spelling—as we'll see below—they're good-value access numbers.
- Silver numbers have 6-7 digits. These make excellent access numbers.
- Gold numbers are 1-5 digits. These high-value Bango Numbers are price-on-application: contact sales@bango.com.

# Bango packages

Each Bango package gives you the right to choose some Bango Numbers, with the more expensive packages giving you more—and shorter—numbers.

Packages are also bundled with random *tracking* Bango Numbers that you don't get to choose (they're allocated automatically by Bango). These are Standard-class numbers that you can use for anything you like—they're best used as internal numbers rather than access numbers.

The more expensive packages let you give some of your numbers Bango Relay and Bango Identifier functionality. Your site developers can use these (with their own coding expertise) to give your site advanced features. For example, they can add personalisation features to your site, and easily charge for multiple pieces of content using the same Bango Number.

Check the Bango web site for details of how many of each type of Bango Number the packages contain when you sign up. Of course, all packages let you buy more Standard, Bronze and Silver numbers, and also more tracking numbers. (The more exclusive Gold numbers are also available.) With the Pro, Focus and Express packages you can buy the right to give more of your numbers Relay or Identifier functionality (not available to buyers of the Micro package).

## Phone spelling: Bango Numbers are also words

With most mobile phones available today, the numbers 2-9 on the keypad select letters of the alphabet when you're writing a text message. The T9 predictive text system in common use even picks the correct letter (eventually, most of the time) from the three or four available on each key.

This means that Bango Numbers are also words. To type the word "dog" in a text message, for example, you press 3 6 4. If you register the Bango Number 364, you're also effectively registering the word "dog" in the Bango system. Since each number corresponds to multiple letters you're also registering the words "fog" and—for fans of The Simpsons—"doh", plus many more three-letter sequences you won't find in the dictionary. But "dog" is *always* 364—the "phone spelling" of dog is 364.

The extremely popular Bango Txt Trigger and Global Txt Trigger services, which we'll cover in Chapter 15, make use of this consistent mapping from words to numbers. With these services a simple text message like "go dog" sent to a particular phone number routes the sender to the URL associated with Bango Number 364.

So the question you need to consider isn't "Which Bango Number is best for my business?" but "Which *word* is best for my business?"

## Making use of your brand

Brands such as product names and company names are a valuable business asset. Many brands bring with them great expectations: the Apple Computer brand, for example, brings with it a rich legacy of award-winning industrial design.

Brand names make excellent Bango Numbers. For example, the UK games provider Groove Gaming registered the Silver Bango Number 476683, which is the phone spelling of the word "Groove". *The Sun* newspaper, published by News Corporation, has gone one better, registering the Gold Bango Number 786—or the word "Sun".

If Gold and Silver numbers are out of your price range, don't worry. The Express package is bundled with two Bronze numbers (8-9 digits) and two Standard numbers (10-50 digits)—many businesses have brand names that long. If not, then you could add another word on the end—for example, "now", "direct" or "mobile". There's no reason you can't find a suitable name—and Bango Number—to fit your price range.

## What service do you provide?

You might want to consider choosing a Bango Number that maps to a more generic word than your specific brand. For example, if you sell background images for phones, would 925572737—the phone spelling for "wallpaper"—be a good investment for you? Someone thinks so: that particular number has already been registered.

Again, you could add more words to end up with a longer Bango Number. For example, you could combine your brand name with the business you're in.

## What's your phone number?

If you don't want a "phone spelling" number, your phone number is an ideal candidate for a Bango Number. It has two excellent qualities: it's long enough, if you include the dialling code, to qualify as a Standard Bango Number; and it's unique to you.

However, the uniqueness only extends to the phone system. Because each digit corresponds to more than one letter of the alphabet in phone spelling, it's possible that someone else has registered that number already—if it maps to an interesting word or words.

## T9 hassles

If you're a regular texter, you'll know that the T9 number-to-text prediction system works well—until two or more valid words have the same phone spelling, like "of" and "me" (both 63), and T9 picks the wrong one. Then the texter has to stop texting and select the alternative word. Or worse, T9 doesn't recognise the word at all and the texter has to switch to an older, more cumbersome entry method.

When choosing a Bango Number based on phone spelling—effectively, choosing a word rather than a number—remember that the Bango Txt Trigger Service uses standard text messages. Your customers will be texting a Bango short code, most probably using a T9-enabled phone.

This means it's important to try out your chosen word on a T9-enabled phone before you commit to the associated Bango Number. See what T9 makes of it!

Ideally T9 will recognise your word. Success.

Occasionally more than one word will fit, and T9 won't pick your word. This is unfortunate, but you might feel it's OK: your word might be too good to change.

Your worst-case scenario is that T9 doesn't recognise your chosen word at all. With some phones this won't be too much of a problem—although you'll see gibberish rather than your word, phone-spelling rules ensure everything still works (the letters displayed still map to the correct digits). However, some phones are fussy. For example, the Sony Ericsson T68i interrupts you when it can't recognise a word and asks you to add it to the dictionary. This is fine if you plan to type the word often, but an irritating inconvenience otherwise. It might even be annoying enough to make some of your potential customers give up before they reach your site. In this case, you might want to think about choosing a different Bango Number.

# Chapter 14
# Simple promotion of your Bango Number

You've decided on your "access" Bango Number—the number you want to promote. If you already have a business or if you're just starting up, an easy next step is to make sure your business promotes that Bango Number in its own materials. In this chapter we'll show how to use the Bango symbol to do that, and how customers can use the Bango Number to access your site.

Before you take any of the steps in this chapter, you must have mapped your chosen Bango Number to your mobile internet site's home page. You do this using the Bango Members' Lounge. To find out more, see Chapter 7.

## The Bango symbol

The Bango symbol, an exclamation mark inside an oval, is intended as a universal identifier for a Bango Number—just as you often see a small image of a telephone next to a phone number. You should always include the Bango symbol immediately before your Bango Number—wherever it appears. This identifies your number as a Bango Number rather than any other kind of number.

Why not just say "Bango" and then give the number? One reason to use the symbol is that it catches the eye—and you want people to notice your number. To a certain extent it also promotes the Bango brand, which could be good for *your* business as well as for Bango.

### Where to find the symbol

At the time of writing, the Bango symbol is available on the Bango web site at http://bango.com/members/marketing/artwork.aspx.

You can download the symbol in red/black or greyscale, in a number of formats:

- TIFF format is best for reducing in size to use on the (fixed or mobile) internet. Almost all image processing applications, such as Paint Shop Pro and Adobe Photoshop, can open TIFF format images. Don't forget to save as GIF or JPEG for use on the web.
- EPS, or Encapsulated PostScript, is a vector image format—which means it can be enlarged as well as reduced. Paint Shop Pro and Adobe PhotoShop (and others) can understand this format too, but will "rasterise" the image—turn it into pixels—at the resolution of your choice, when you open the image. Typically you'd use this format if you need a large symbol and the TIFF format doesn't give you the results you need.
- Adobe Illustrator format is another vector image format, used by the product of the same name. Adobe Illustrator doesn't rasterise the image: it's a vector-based drawing application. Use this format if you need to produce a vector-based image that includes the Bango symbol, for example.

## Bango symbol do's and don'ts

- Always use the best quality symbol you can. This means the two-colour symbol in most cases, such on web sites or with four-colour printing. For one-colour printing, use the greyscale version (which is actually just black and white, with no grey).
- To use the symbol on the web, reduce the image to the size of the surrounding text. We recommend you resize to no smaller than about 15 pixels to avoid the symbol turning into a smudge.
- The symbol is a trademark of Bango, so you're not allowed to "abuse" it in any way. This means you mustn't recolour it or distort it, no matter how much you might be tempted. Similarly, you mustn't include the symbol as part of your own logo.
- The symbol won't work very well on a dark background: the black surround will disappear. Use a light-coloured background, preferably white or near-white.

- Where you can't use the symbol—for example, in a text-only medium—then use an exclamation mark instead.

## Where to promote your Bango Number

As a rule of thumb, display the Bango symbol with your Bango Number wherever you currently display your phone or fax number, or web address. Here are some ideas:

- On your (fixed internet) web site. Browsers or customers can spot the Bango symbol, and go to their phones to access your mobile internet site using the Bango Number.

- On your existing mobile internet site. You might have a mobile version of your web site already, set up before you started using Bango services. It's still worth promoting your Bango Number there. Don't forget to make the reference a hypertext link. If you're worried about reproducing the Bango symbol at a small size, consider using an exclamation mark instead.

- On your printed materials. This includes brochures, mailouts, press advertisements and letterheads.

## The user experience

As a content provider you want to make sure your *user experience* is as good as it can be. The easier it is for customers to access your site—even before they try to buy any content—the better their overall user experience will be.

Let's compare the main methods a potential customer can use to access your site from their mobile phone, assuming they've seen an advert using the Bango symbol with your Bango Number.

### Using the Bango mobile site

Andy starts a WAP session on his mobile phone. Once connected, he types in the URL bango.net (different phones let you do this in different ways) and waits for the page.

The Bango web site detects that Andy's using a mobile phone, and displays a page optimised for phones.

Andy types the Bango Number into the box, and selects Go There. In this example, Andy's entered the Bango Number for National Rail in the UK (notice that 87246, a Gold Bango Number, is phone spelling for the word "train").

The Bango system translates the Bango Number to the URL http://wap.nationalrail.co.uk, and forwards Andy to that page.

The most time-consuming part of the process is typing in the URL bango.net. Andy could improve his user experience a great deal by bookmarking that URL rather than typing it each time. (Of course, he could bookmark the destination URL—National Rail—instead of the bango.net URL, if he never needs to access another site using a Bango Number.)

## Using an operator portal

At least twenty mobile networks around the world include a a link to Bango on their mobile internet home pages or on a navigation or search page. These so-called *operator portals* help over 60 million users world-wide access content quickly.

Operator portals typically show the link as "!Bango" or "!number", and sometimes include the Bango symbol, as shown here. Users just select that link and jump to the Bango home page.

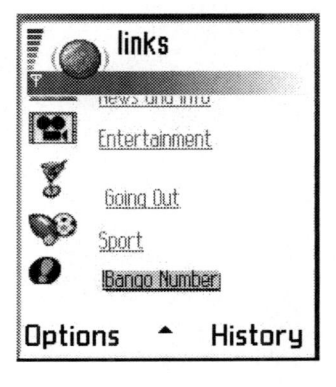

For phones preconfigured with an operator portal, this can be a reasonably straightforward user experience.

# Effectiveness

In business collateral like web pages, brochures and the sides of vehicles, the Bango symbol and Bango Number combination is unlikely to be any more effective than your phone number or web site address.

The primary reason is a "disconnect". A good analogy is to imagine someone spotting a URL on a passing taxi. Unless they're looking out of the window of a cybercafe or a wireless-enabled coffee shop, they're unlikely to have an internet-connected web browser to hand to immediately visit that site. Instead they have to take some immediate action—remember the URL—and then take another action later—visit the URL.

With a Bango Number on a brochure, there's a similar problem. Even if the person has a WAP-enabled mobile phone on them (most people do these days), they have to start a WAP session, go to the Bango web site (using a bookmark or operator portal, or by typing the URL), and then enter the number. It's a multi-stage process, which always reduces the effectiveness of a promotional campaign.

That's not to say that this approach will be completely *ineffective*—if that were true then businesses wouldn't put phone numbers on their letterheads. However, you're likely to find the promotional techniques described in following chapters much more effective at attracting and retaining paying customers.

Chapter 15

# The Bango Txt Trigger and Web Trigger services

The Bango Txt Trigger Service is a simple but extremely popular—and profitable—way to attract customers to your site. Customers don't need to know anything about Bango Numbers or visit the Bango web site: they arrive at your site with money to spend.

In this chapter we'll describe this service, which is free to all Bango content providers. We'll show you how to promote your mobile shop using the service and what your customers will experience when they use it. We'll also describe how you can use the Global Txt Trigger Service, bringing customers from around the world to your site.

The Bango Web Trigger service helps you promote your mobile site from your fixed internet web site. With this service, users simply fill in their phone number on your web site and receive a WAP Push message directing them to your mobile site.

## Overview

SMS texting is incredibly popular around the world. In the UK an average of 82 million text messages are sent every day—and 133 million texts were sent on New Year's Day 2005. Texting shows no sign of losing its popularity, especially among teens and twentysomethings. And the same people who like texting are also keen buyers of mobile internet content, so it's no surprise that Bango decided to bring these two worlds together with the Bango Txt Trigger Service.

Put simply, the service allows any mobile phone user in the UK to send a short text message to Bango and be automatically redirected to a mobile internet site. They're registered in the Bango system if necessary and the cost of the text message—£1.50—is immediately credited to their Bango account, to spend on any Bango-billed mobile internet content.

For your potential customers, sending a text is quick and easy. And you can promote your service in terms your customers already understand. It's an ideal "call to action" in all marketing collateral—posters, magazines, billboards, web sites and so on.

At the moment the Bango Txt Trigger Service is only available in the UK. It can be used with all network providers except Virgin (Virgin customers can still access mobile internet sites but must use other methods to access them.)

To attract customers outside the UK, subscribers to the Pro package can use the Global Txt Trigger Service, described later in this chapter.

## How to promote your site

In Chapter 13 we described phone spelling and explained that the best Bango Numbers to use to promote your site are those that map to words on a standard mobile phone handset. For example, the Hollywood Reloaded site in Chapter 7 has the access Bango Number 46559966373562333, which maps to the word "hollywoodreloaded".

Don't forget that the shorter, the better. Your company might be called "Totally Fabulous Ringtones" but think how long that would take to type on a keypad! Bango Numbers that map to a short word or phrase, like "Fabtones", are much better—especially those that are easy to type using T9 predictive text.

With the Bango Txt Trigger Service you use the word form of your Bango Number to promote your site. In your promotional material you tell users to text the message go `your-word`—for example, go `hollywoodreloaded`—to a Bango-operated *short code* (five-digit phone number).

To promote a U-rated site, use the short code 83055. For R-rated sites, use a 69xxx or 89xxx short code (see Chapter 8 for more information, and check the Members' Lounge for an up-to-date list of Bango short codes).

Subscribers to the Pro package can also use the Bango Free Txt Trigger Service, where the content provider pays for the cost of the WAP Push message—see the Members' Lounge for details. And there's also the Global Txt Trigger Service, which can be used worldwide, and the Web Trigger Service, which takes users straight from your fixed internet site to your mobile shop. We'll describe these below.

When promoting your site, remember to keep your message *simple* and *clear*. Make your call to action really stand out: for our Hollywood Reloaded site, we might say "Text **go hollywoodreloaded** to **83055** for news and gossip, 25x7", with the "go" message and the short code highlighted in colour.

For example, Manchester United Football Club uses the Bango Number 6832—which maps to the initials MUFC—to advertise its mobile internet service in many different media, such as match programmes and its fixed internet web site, using a Bango Txt Trigger.

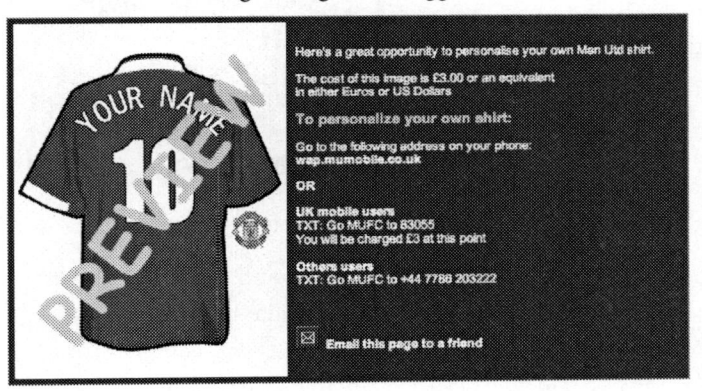

<image>
Preview image of a Manchester United shirt personalisation page:

Here's a great opportunity to personalise your own Man Utd shirt.
The cost of this image is £3.00 or an equivalent in either Euros or US Dollars

To personalize your own shirt:

Go to the following address on your phone:
wap.mumobile.co.uk

OR

UK mobile users
TXT: Go MUFC to 83055
You will be charged £3 at this point

Others users
TXT: Go MUFC to +44 7788 203222

✉ Email this page to a friend
</image>

You don't need to publish a catalogue to advertise your mobile shop. Anywhere you currently include your URL you can also include the "go" message. Don't forget to add it to your fixed internet site too: many people don't realise that web sites they visit from their PC are also available—with content to buy—on the mobile internet.

If your Bango Number doesn't map to a recognisable word or phrase, you can still use the Bango Txt Trigger Service: tell users to text go your-number—for example, go 46559966373562333—to 83055 or an R-rated short code instead.

You must make sure you comply with telecommunications codes of practice. You can find full details in Appendix 3, but one important point to note is that when using a premium-rate short code, you *must* mention the cost of the message. If you don't follow the guidelines in Appendix 3, then the regulator ICSTIS has the power to fine you.

Bango strongly recommends that you contact Bango Customer Services *before* starting any promotional campaign to ensure that you're using the correct short code and that your message meets the current guidelines.

## User experience

Let's use the example of our Hollywood Reloaded site from Chapter 7. For a more in-depth description of the user experience that also covers paying for content, see the *Typical user experience* section in that chapter.

Griff sees a poster at his local cinema advertising the Hollywood Reloaded site. The advert tells him to text go hollywoodreloaded to 83055. He does so, causing £1.50 to appear on his next phone bill. At the same time he's registered with the Bango system as a new user, and his £1.50 is used to top up his Bango account with money to spend on content.

Shortly afterwards Griff receives a text message from Bango that confirms the transaction and asks him to wait for another "auto-redirect" message. This second message—a "WAP Push" message—is a semi-automatic way to start a WAP session and go to a specific mobile internet site. Griff sees a "service message" (which is how some phones describe a WAP Push message), reads it, and selects the option that takes him directly to the Hollywood Reloaded site.

Griff can now spend his £1.50 credit on our site or on any other Bango-enabled site. He can bookmark Hollywood Reloaded if he wants: he doesn't need to use the Bango Txt Trigger again (but it's a handy way of topping up his account with £1.50 if he wants to).

Note that if Griff mistypes the "go" message—for example, if he types the word-equivalent of a Bango Number that's not in use, or if he omits the "go"—he'll still be charged £1.50 and be credited with that amount on Bango's systems.

# Contacting your customers

Every Bango Txt Trigger sent by a mobile phone user also includes their phone number. This information is stored on the Bango systems along with all other customer data, such as what they've bought. This is important data for you as a content provider: it's your customer base.

All Bango packages—Pro, Focus, Express and Micro—allow you to find out who's used your Bango Txt Trigger and then bought content from you. The data you receive associates customer phone numbers with Bango Numbers used for purchasing content.

You can then use this data for marketing promotions, as long as you comply with the Privacy and Electronic Communications Regulations 2003—the anti-spamming law that came into effect on December 11 2003.

If you're planning to contact your customers we strongly recommend you consult your legal advisor first to check that your plans comply with the law. Here's a rough guide (not legal advice!) to what you can and can't do:

- You can send email or SMS text marketing messages for similar services to existing customers, without their explicit consent. This means you can continue to draw customers back to your mobile internet site with news and offers.

- You must not market any other services to customers unless you get their permission (they need to opt in to such services). It's a good idea to solicit this permission from users while they visit your mobile internet site. You'll need to use the Bango Identifier Service to identify the user and record their agreement (see Chapter 10).

- You must provide a way for customers to opt out of further marketing *every time* you contact them. There should be no charge for this—only the standard cost of sending the opt-out message.

If you want to contact your customers but don't know where to start, Bango can run a text marketing campaign for you. You'll need to pay for each text message you send and there's an overall fee for the campaign. Contact Bango for more information about this service.

Note that Bango can only supply details of customers who used a Bango Txt Trigger to access your site. Customers who used other access methods—

direct entry of Bango Numbers on operator portals, for instance—can't be identified in this way.

## The Global Txt Trigger Service

At the moment the Bango Txt Trigger Service is only available in the UK. If you subscribe to the Pro package, however, you can use the *Global Txt Trigger* Service to attract customers from all over the world.

The Global Txt Trigger Service uses a simple text message go your-word, just like the UK-only service. However, the message must be sent to a international phone number: +44 7786 203222 (+44 is the international dialling code for the UK). Use the same phone number no matter where your content is located.

There's a much more important difference: as not all countries have Premium SMS services, the user *is not charged* except for the standard cost on their network for sending a text message (which goes on their bill as normal, and is unrelated to your site or the Bango system). However, the cost of the WAP Push message the user receives to bring them to your site must still be covered: with the Global Txt Trigger Service, the *content provider* pays.

To pay for these messages, you buy a number of *Txt Credits* from Bango and assign them against the Bango Number you want to promote using the Global Txt Trigger. Each time a user sends a Global Txt Trigger some of these credits are deducted. Currently each response costs you six Txt Credits (12p). Check the Members' Lounge for current Txt Credit rates.

You'll be notified when your Txt Credits are getting low. If you run out, then users won't receive the WAP Push message when they send a Global Txt Trigger.

Also, it's worth noting that the Global Txt Trigger Service *doesn't* register customers with the Bango system—this will happen the first time they buy content.

## The Bango Web Trigger Service

The Bango Txt Trigger Service and the Bango Global Txt Trigger Service are ideal for non-interactive media: magazine copy or advertisements, billboards, and so on. But your web site is interactive! It would be great if you could short-cut the process by collecting a web surfer's phone number and pushing their mobile phone direct to your valuable content.

That's what the Bango Web Trigger Service helps you do. You simply add a form field to your web site in which users can type their phone number. The server-side script that processes the form sends the number to Bango, together with other information, and Bango sends a WAP Push that takes users to your site plus a confirmation text message back to the user's phone: wherever they are in the world. Bango customers such as *The Sun* use this service to turn web site readers into ringtone buyers, for example.

With this service, the user is not charged. As with the Global Txt Trigger Service, you need to purchase a number of Txt Credits from Bango to cover the cost of the messages sent to each user. Currently each WAP Push plus confirmation costs six Txt Credits: check the Members' Lounge for any changes to these rates.

The Bango Web Trigger Service is available to subscribers to the Pro and Focus packages.

Since the Bango Web Trigger Service involves your web site, you need to include some code on the site to collect the user's phone number and sent it to Bango. For full details of how to do this, see the Members' Lounge.

## Effectiveness

There's no doubt that the Bango Txt Trigger is a highly effective way to promote your site. It's simple for you to describe and simple for customers to use. There are some—very sensible—terms and conditions, such as ensuring your customers know in advance how much the "go" message will cost. And customers arrive with at least £1.50 credit available to spend on your site.

You should consider using Bango Txt Triggers as the primary way to advertise your site in all your collateral.

For Pro customers, the Global Txt Trigger Service helps you tap into the global market quickly and easily. Although you bear an additional cost for this service, the dramatically larger market can more than offset any disadvantages.

## Chapter 16
# Viral marketing

Most people consider Hotmail the first—and some say finest—example of viral marketing. It grew almost entirely as the result of a one-line message inserted at the end of every piece of email sent by an existing Hotmail customer: "Get your private, free email at http://www.hotmail.com". As more mail was sent from Hotmail, more people saw that message and signed up. And so even more mail was sent from Hotmail.

Hotmail is the nirvana of viral marketing: the ideal state that everyone aspires to. In this chapter we'll look at what viral marketing can do, and what it can't do, for your mobile shop.

## What is viral marketing?

A virus replicates from host to host. As the infected population grows it can start to expand exponentially: in a short time, everyone's infected. That's the intent of viral marketing: to infect everyone with an idea or a product by starting small and relying on human nature to spread the word.

The film *The Blair Witch Project* reputedly had a tiny marketing budget. It relied entirely on word of mouth to advertise itself, helped by a small web site that could feed the interest at very little cost.

Some key words and phrases associated with viral marketing:

- **Word of mouth.** Personal recommendation is the best advertising money can't buy. But be aware: a *dis*recommendation—a negative review—spreads just as virulently. Friends influence friends both positively and negatively.

- **Worth talking about.** Gossip moves faster than light; the daily grind just doesn't have the same allure. American journalist John B. Bogart said it best: "When a dog bites a man, that is not news, because it happens so often. But if a man bites a dog, that is news."

- **Cheap.** That is, cheap relative to the equivalent return through non-viral marketing. You *do* have to spend money to make money, but with good viral marketing your investment buys the magic beans not the beanstalk.

- **Exponential.** Place a penny on the top-left square of a chessboard, two pennies on the next square, four on the next, and so on—doubling the amount with each square. By the 64th square you'd be placing, uh, a little (a lot?) over 9,000,000,000,000,000,000 pennies. This is exponential growth. Viral marketing can't bring you that many pennies in revenue, sadly. But it suggests that if you tell one person something, and that person tells two others (who haven't already been told), and so on, you can—in theory—quickly reach almost everyone.

## Viral marketing myths

Viral marketing can help your business grow a loyal customer base with only a relatively small outlay. But there are some things that viral marketing can't do.

- **It can't sell a bad product.** Even the best viral marketing programmes are scuppered if the product doesn't come up to scratch. The viral effect might work—word might spread quickly—but it might be a negative message.

- **It can't sell a good product to the wrong market.** As we said in Chapter 12: you must know who your customers are. Viral marketing isn't a magic trick you can use to force people to buy a product they don't want.

- **Exponential growth never happens.** The social networks in which we live are often near-islands, almost isolated from one another. A message moving virally amongst a group of friends needs to escape from that network and into other networks to survive and grow. There are also networks of networks (analagous the group of businesses in the same industry) that can slow growth at a higher level. This "clumping" of networks (and networks of networks, and so on) helps explain why growth is always less than the theoretical maximum. However, there are clues here to allow us to better target our marketing: see below.

- **Viral marketing is not spam.** Spam is unsolicited email (or faxes, or text messages, or paper mail, or cold-calling). Viral marketing is often unsolicited, but almost always involves someone you know and trust.

## The Tipping Point

Every student of viral marketing should read *The Tipping Point* by Malcolm Gladwell (http://www.gladwell.com/books.html). The author says on his web site:

"It's a book about change. In particular, it's a book that presents a new way of understanding why change so often happens as quickly and as unexpectedly as it does. For example, why did crime drop so dramatically in New York City in the mid-1990s? How does a novel written by an unknown author end up a national bestseller? Why do teens smoke in greater and greater numbers, when every single person in the country knows that cigarettes kill? Why is word-of-mouth so powerful? What makes TV shows like Sesame Street so good at teaching kids how to read? I think the answer to all those questions is the same. It's that ideas and behavior and messages and products sometimes behave just like outbreaks of infectious disease. They are social epidemics. *The Tipping Point* is an examination of the social epidemics that surround us." (http://www.gladwell.com/books2.html)

The book describes three special types of people, each crucial in their own way to starting a "word-of-mouth epidemic":

- **Connectors** know lots of people. They bridge gaps between separate social groups: they help ideas pass between otherwise independent networks. According to Gladwell, everyone knows a connector—but very few of us are connectors ourselves.
- **Mavens** accumulate knowledge and want to communicate it. Gladwell says, "They read more magazines than the rest of us, more newspapers, and they may be the only people who read junk mail." They educate those around them, almost compulsively, and people trust what they say and take their advice.

- **Salesmen** are persuaders. They persuade both verbally and non-verbally: by their body language, subtle nods and smiles. Studies have shown that their charm, enthusiasm and energy are almost infectious.

Identifying connectors, mavens and salesmen can help your message spread more effectively, working around the network clumpiness that hinders growth. They may make the difference between a successful viral marketing campaign and an unsuccessful one.

## Send to a friend

A *Send to a friend* link is a great way to increase your revenue by making it easier for customers to recommend your content to others—the most effective publicity you can receive.

The Bango Service includes an easy-to-use send-to-a-friend mechanism. On your mobile internet site, you simply include a link to a Bango URL, quoting the Bango Number of your site. Here's an example that uses the Bango Number 1234:

```
<p>Like this site?
<a href="http://bango.net/sendfriend.aspx?sendbango=1234">Tell a friend!</a></p>
```

When someone clicks the "Tell a friend!" link, they'll see a page on the Bango web site that lets them type the phone number of their friend, in international format (as long as there's an SMS service, the friend could be anywhere from Aberdeen to the Antarctic!). They can also include a short message and their own name or phone number. Sending the message costs them 20p (converted to their local currency if necessary).

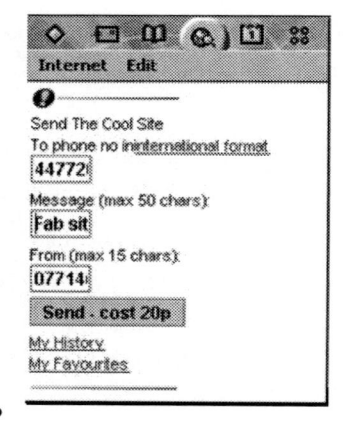

The friend receives a text message and a WAP Push that takes them to your site, just as if they'd used a Bango Txt Trigger (or Global Txt Trigger). Unlike with the Bango Txt Trigger Service, the friend pays nothing.

The Bango Number you use for a send-to-a-friend link must be an access number, and there must be *no charge* attached to that number.

# Examples

In this section we'll give some simple examples of viral marketing that you may be able to use or adapt for your mobile internet site.

## Prize competitions

Offering a desirable prize in a competition can often draw customers to your site. As word spreads about the prize—assuming it's good news—you'll gain publicity by association.

A prize doesn't have to be substantial or truly expensive. You could offer the winner free content from your site for a month, for instance. But you may find a quirky or rare prize attracts more entrants, and more publicity.

## eCards

An eCard is an electronic greetings card. Many sites use free eCards to attract visitors. They let you send eCards to anyone by email, selecting the "front cover" of the card from a range of images, and including your own message. Along with the card (or a link to your web site where the card can be viewed) you'd include a short note explaining where the sender found the eCard—on your site.

## Videos

How many times has a friend sent you a humorous video file—or a link to one—by email? These videos are another type of viral marketing. Some companies specialise in making viral marketing videos, which are short, funny, tell a story and sell a product. They're designed to be forwarded by email, or to attract links from other sites.

You can find many examples of viral videos on the internet: there are sites devoted to collecting them.

## Linkable content

Linkable content is designed to persuade people to reference it on their own site. For example, a controversial or rare interview with a notable name can attract hordes of additional visitors as word spreads through online news portals.

Also, search engines such as Google rate sites more highly the more people link to them. The higher the rating, the better placement in search results.

## Effectiveness

Viral marketing is an art not a science. It *can* be extremely effective: we've seen how films such as *The Blair Witch Project* became well-known purely through viral marketing. However, there are no guarantees. The key, as ever, is to know your customers. If you can find an approach that works—that attracts the connectors, mavens and salesmen of your target market—then you may find that viral marketing gives you a great return on your investment.

It's certainly worthwhile adding Bango's send-to-a-friend functionality to your site. It costs you nothing, and could help spread the word about your site to anyone, anywhere.

Chapter 17
# The Bango Directory and World of Content

In this chapter we'll talk about the Bango Directory and the Bango World of Content web site. With hundreds of thousands of visits per month, the Bango Directory is an important promotional tool that can attract thousands of potential and returning customers to your site. Improving your position in the directory could be key to the growth of your site. The Bango Directory is the source for the Bango World of Content web site, for users searching and browsing for mobile content using the fixed internet.

## What is the Bango Directory?

The Bango Directory is a list of Bango Numbers, each associated with a description and a number of keywords. With each Bango Number you buy you're given the right to add that number to the Bango Directory, with the description and keywords of your choice.

Potential customers search the Bango Directory using keywords. The search engine uses a number of criteria, which we'll describe below—and which you can influence in various ways—to choose the order in which Bango Numbers appear.

There are some limitations to be aware of:

- You can include two descriptions. One is limited to 100 characters, and is displayed to people searching from their mobile phone. The other description can be as long as 300 characters, and is displayed to people searching from the fixed internet.
- You can select up to five keywords.

New Bango Directory entries—and changes to existing entries—are reviewed by Bango staff before they appear in the directory. The reviewers check for:

- **Accuracy.** Your description must match the content of your site.
- **Functionality.** The site works in the formats you've specified (WML, HTML, and so on).
- **Suitability.** The entry must conform to the Bango Directory terms and conditions. For example, you mustn't say anything defamatory or discriminatory in the entry or in your site itself.

Once an entry has been added or edited in the Bango Directory, it's also immediately available to fixed internet surfers on the Bango World of Content web site.

## Adding your site to the Bango Directory

You use the Bango Members' Lounge to manage your Bango Directory entry: to write your description and to choose your keywords. You also use this site to enter bids for keyword auctions, which we'll discuss later in this chapter.

To add, modify or delete an entry in the Bango Directory, first go to the Members' Lounge in your web browser and log in. Then go to the Manage Content section to see all the Bango Numbers in your Bango package (if you have more than one package click the appropriate Edit Numbers button to see its Bango Numbers).

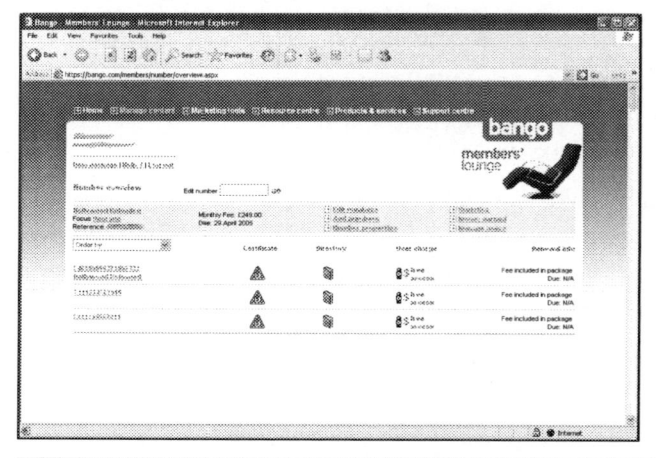

Each Bango Number in the list has an icon in the Directory column. The icon shows whether the directory entry for that number is accepted (in the directory), pending (needs to be reviewed by Bango staff) or not present.

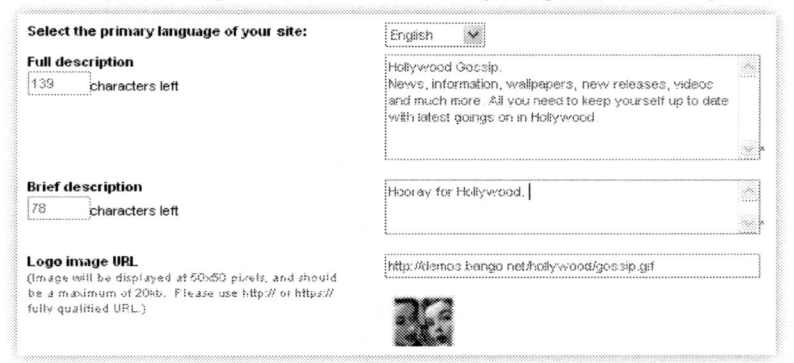

To add, modify or delete the Bango Directory entry for a number, click the icon. The page you'll see shows you the current entry if any. Change the details and click Submit; or to delete the directory entry, click Delete.

## Selecting appropriate keywords

You're limited to five keywords for each Bango Number you own. Here are some tips for choosing the most useful keywords.

- **People search for new content using general terms.** Our Hollywood site includes gossip articles and celebrity photos. Keywords like `gossip`, `rumours`, `photos`, `celebrities` and `stars` all describe our site generically. A site with downloadable videos might use the keyword `3gp`—the video format they support. People often search for these general terms—but that means lots of entries in the Bango Directory also use these terms. You need to use them, but you may need to use other techniques to improve your position in the search results.

- **People search for what they've seen before using specific terms.** This usually means your brand: in our case this might be `hollywood` (although that's arguably a general term too). People search for brands when they've visited the site before, remember the site's name, but can't remember how they reached the site.

- **People hate finding sites that don't relate to their search terms.** Don't waste any of your valuable search keywords by using what you believe are popular search terms that are unrelated to your site. Although we could use the popular keywords `ringtones` and `games` for our Hollywood site to try to attract more visitors, there are no ringtones or games on the site. This will annoy visitors, drive them away, and generate negative word-of-mouth (see Chapter 16).

## How search results are ranked

The Bango Directory search engine uses a number of criteria to decide how to rank the search results. For each entry in the Bango Directory, the search engine applies the criteria to generate a total "score" for the entry, and then displays the results ordered by score.

Some prime locations are reserved for auction-winners—see the next section—but for all other spots, these are the criteria that apply:

- **The search terms.** Naturally! If a user searches for `java games`, the results will include entries that contain the keywords `java` and/or `games`.

- **Keyword position.** If a user searches for `ringtones`, then entries with `ringtones` as the first keyword will score higher than entries with `ringtones` as the second (or later) keyword. Tip: put your general keywords first, and your specific keywords—such as your site name—last (usually only your site's directory entry will use your site name, so you don't need a high score for that keyword).

- **Language.** The Bango system automatically detects the language a user's phone is configured to use. In your entry in the Bango Directory you can set the language your keywords are using. The search engine will give a bonus score to entries that match the user's language.

- **Device type.** The Bango system also detects the device a user's accessing the Bango Directory with, and gives bonus points for sites available for that device. For example, mobile internet sites will score more highly when a user searches the Bango Directory from a mobile phone.

- **Popularity.** The more times someone has visited a site using the Bango Number (either directly or using a Bango Txt Trigger), the more points it will score. Popular sites "bubble up" the search results.

- **Phone spelling.** If the Bango Number of an entry is a phone spelling of a search term, the entry receives a bonus score. For example, the owner of the Bango Number 42637—the phone spelling of the word "games"—receives bonus points when someone searches for `games`.

## "Top 4" keyword auctions

Pole position in the search results for a keyword—or at least, somewhere in the first few positions—can help drive potential customers to your site. Bango reserves the first four positions in the search results for the most popular keywords for the highest bidders in an auction process. (All other search results are ranked purely using the scoring system above.)

Auctions take place regularly—usually every month. There are separate auctions for each keyword, and for each of the top four positions for that keyword. Positions for ten keywords are auctioned in total: five U-rated keywords (currently `ringtones`, `free`, `games`, `chat` and `logos`) and five R-rated keywords (currently `porn`, `sex`, `hardcore`, `gay` and `adult`).

If you win one of the auctions, your site will appear in the appropriate search results until the next auction for that position.

To bid in a keyword auction, or simply to find out when the next auctions take place, log in to the Members' Lounge at http://bango.com/members, then go to the Marketing Tools section and click Content Directory.

Bango auctions include an "autobid" feature. This lets you specify the *maximum* amount you want to pay for a particular keyword. The Bango system will automatically bid the minimum bid price on your behalf; if someone else bids more than you, your bid is automatically increased—to £5 above the opposing bid—as long as your maximum bid hasn't been exceeded. If someone bids more than your maximum bid, you can always bid again manually or by increasing your autobid.

## User experience

How does a potential customer search the directory? Let's follow DJ as he looks for ringtones for his phone.

DJ starts a WAP session and chooses his bookmark for http://bango.net. On the Bango page he selects the "Search Directory" link.

DJ now needs to choose whether to search U-rated content or all content. If he selects "Search all content" the Bango system will not let him proceed if his phone is barred from accessing R-rated content—see Chapter 8 for more information. Here DJ selects "Search U rated content".

Now DJ could type "ringtones" in the box, but he instead selects "Hot searches" as he suspects that many people will be searching for ringtones. He's right: he selects "ringtones" on the next page.

DJ can now select any of the ten content providers listed, choose to list the next ten search results, or select "Search Again". He selects the first content provider on the list, which displays the 100-character description written by the content provider along with a link to the site. DJ selects this link and can now browse the site and, if he finds anything he likes, buy some ringtones.

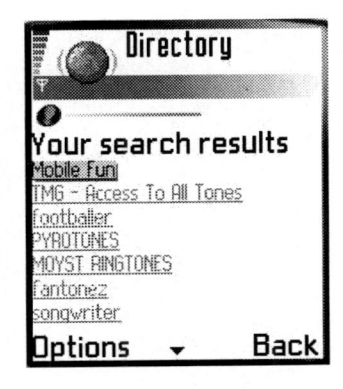

If DJ were surfing from his PC, he could use the Bango World of Content web site to see what's in the Bango Directory. The URL is the same as for mobile access—http://bango.net—but the content is tailored for fixed internet users. Starting from the World of Content home page DJ can search for content by keyword, or jump quickly to hot searches or state-of-the-art sites.

# Chapter 18
# Charging your customers

In previous chapters we've talked about the various methods you can use to attract people to your mobile internet site—the promotion of your access Bango Number. In this chapter we'll discuss the next step: charging customers for access to your valuable content. We'll explain the charging options available to you (including a subscription service), give you tips on how much to charge, and also cover currency issues.

See also Appendix 4 to find out how the Bango system takes payment from your customers.

## What parts of the site should remain free?

You may be tempted to charge for everything. After all, you want to make as much money as you can from your site. But this is a dangerous tactic: how many shops on your local high street charge for access? How many charge for browsing bookshelves or clothing racks? Shopping on the mobile internet isn't that much different from shopping on foot. Some parts of your mobile shop should be freely available:

- **The home page.** If a potential customer can't see any part of your site without paying, they probably won't pay. (You may ask: doesn't a potential customer pay £1.50 to access a site from a Bango Txt Trigger? Yes and no. The charge goes on the customer's phone bill, but the money doesn't go to the site: it goes to the customer's Bango account, and can be spent on any Bango-enabled site.)

- **Freebies, teasers and thumbnails.** Potential customers like to try before they buy. Giving them free access to thumbnails, with one or two free images, gives them enough confidence in the quality of your content to be happy purchasing more of it. Teasers—enticing headlines, for example—act in a similar way.

- **Bookmarkable "hooks".** In our Hollywood example, we included a page listing upcoming movie releases. This is another "hook" into the site—prime bookmarkable content. As long as you update the page regularly, customers will bookmark it as a reliable source of information. Our simple example could be extended much further. For example, we could make each film title a link to a separate cast list page on our site, with links from there to chargeable content such as photos of the stars.

## What should I charge for?

As always, start with the customer. In our Hollywood example our customer is probably in their teens or twenties, interested in the stars of the movies and Hollywood generally—sometimes even more than the movies themselves. This means our site charges for content primarily about people—the gossip articles and the photos—rather than content about films.

Our gossip articles are also pieces of content not easily found elsewhere. Exclusive information like this is valuable, chargeable content. So is niche information relevant to a specific sport or hobby, such as content about a particular football club. Although niches are by definition smaller markets, those markets contain a higher proportion of people willing to spend money in the niche area. Fans of a film star or sporting hero will often pay for almost anything related to that person, for example. The better you target your customer, the easier it is to know what they'll pay for.

Don't underestimate the value of the *service* associated with the content. For example, photos of Hollywood stars are available everywhere from newspapers to fixed internet web sites. But those photos are hard to transfer to a phone to use as wallpaper. Our Hollywood site performs a valuable service: it resizes images to fit certain phone screens. That service is something that people are happy to pay for.

The most valuable content for a mobile user is content that's immediately relevant to them while they're on the move. If you can answer a question like "where's the nearest…?" or "how do I get to…?" on your site, then charge for the answers. Location-based services like these are ideal chargeable content.

You might think that old images are worthless, but they're not. Archives of older material are often a treasure-trove of valuable content—often by completists looking for that one elusive picture.

## Charging options

The Bango Service includes three main charging options. You choose one of the options for each Bango Number you use for charging. (There's another option, the Bango Txt Subscription Service, described later in this chapter.)

If you decide to use more than one of the charging options on your site, we recommend you take special care to make this clear on the site.

The following sections explain the options available, and the type of content that suits each option best.

### Single access

With this option you charge a specific fee for each access to the content.

This option is best for "browse and buy" mobile shops—sites that most resemble the high-street experience. Your customers already understand how to pay for goods this way from "real life" so there's no learning curve.

Perhaps due to its familiarity, this option is the most popular charging method.

### Multiple accesses

With this option you charge a specific fee for a certain number of accesses to the content. You decide how many accesses are allowed.

This option is useful for image archive sites where Bango Relay functionality is used to charge for access to the archive. You could charge, say, 50p for any ten images.

### Timed access

With this option you charge a specific fee for unlimited access to the content for a certain time period (of your choice).

This option is useful for chat sites, and for searching or browsing lists that are themselves valuable (such as a list of nearby restaurants). It's also another way you could charge for access to your archives.

## The Bango Txt Subscription Service

The charging options in the previous section are available to all Bango customers. For subscribers to the Pro package, there's another option: the *Bango Txt Subscription Service*. This service is available at no extra cost, and can help you maximize your revenue through automatic, recurring payments.

Like the timed-access charging mechanism, the Bango Txt Subscription Service gives users unlimited access to content within a certain time period. The difference is that users *subscribe* to this access. At the start of each subscription period they're charged, taken *automatically* to the content, and have access to that content for the subscription period. And naturally, you can then direct them to the other content on your site—so not only do you receive regular payments from the subscribers, you also have the opportunity to gain extra revenue from your other content.

Users sign up to, and opt out of, the subscription using simple text messages: by texting `start word` or `end word` to 83055 (or an R-rated short code), where `word` is the word form of a Bango Number (just as with the Bango Txt Trigger Service described in Chapter 15).

The user's subscription starts immediately. They're billed the appropriate amount (a multiple of £1.50) and receive a WAP Push message that takes them to the content. Like the Bango Txt Trigger Service, the subscription charge is credited to their Bango account. Unlike the Bango Txt Trigger Service, the cost of the content is then automatically deducted.

Within the subscription period—normally a day, but the duration is up to you—they have unlimited access to this content. At the end of the subscription period, they automatically receive another WAP Push to the content, and are charged again. The cycle repeats until the user unsubscribes with the `end` message. (After unsubscribing, users have access to the content for the remainder of the current subscription period.)

Like the Bango Txt Trigger Service, the Bango Txt Subscription Service is currently available only within the UK.

## Setting up the service

To set up the Bango Txt Subscription Service you need to contact Bango Technical Support. With their help you:

- Agree to some supplementary terms and conditions.
- Choose and set up the Bango Number, including content charges and the duration of the subscription period (one day or longer, but it's recommended you keep subscription periods to no more than a month).

Currently you can't set up this service yourself within the Bango Members' Lounge.

Once you've set up the service you can then start promoting to your users. You can use the same promotional techniques as for the Bango Txt Trigger Service. Ensure you make the charges and the length of the subscription period clear in your promotional materials. For example, "Subscription costs £1.50 per day and can be stopped at any time".

## Ideas

The Bango Txt Subscription Service is great for bringing people to your site regularly. But people want some bang for their buck-fifty. They'll keep the subscription running if they receive valuable content in return. If the site is unchanged and the content stale, they'll quickly unsubscribe.

Here are some ideas for subscription content:

- A "cool image of the day".
- Daily news and gossip.
- A new ringtone each week.
- A game or video of the week.

Make sure that there's an easy route from the subscription content to the rest of your site: you want people to browse your other content and buy that too. Treat the subscription content as the entry point to your site: users should *start* here, not *finish* here.

To cater for users who return within the subscription period (for example by following the WAP Push message again), you could introduce an element of randomness to the content. If users begin to expect new, interesting content every visit, they'll visit—and buy—more often. There's plenty of scope for experimentation.

Remember that users are charged £1.50 (or a multiple) each subscription period, no matter what the cost of the subscription content. If your subscription content costs £1, then the excess 50p for each subscription period remains in their Bango account to spend on any Bango-enabled content. It's a good idea for the subscription content to cost the same as the regular subscription charge to avoid the balance building up in the user's Bango account. All those excess 50p's soon add up!

## How much to charge?

When deciding how much to charge, consider the following:

- How much would your customers be prepared to pay?
- What is the content worth?
- Are the customers getting value for money?
- How does the content compare to other media?
- How can you charge obsessive users more money?

It's difficult to give exact guidelines but smaller amounts—no more than £1 or £2—generally work best. You should aim to grow a large volume of returning customers, each paying small amounts for content. People are happy to make multiple *micropayments* almost without stopping to think, but will hesitate before paying a single larger amount—even if the total of their micropayments exceeds it.

The Bango system lets you charge as little as 1p (or 1c) for any item of content, though in practice you may want to charge no less than 10p (or 10c).

## Using the Members' Lounge to set charges

You choose the charging option and set the charges for each Bango Number within the Members' Lounge web site. Here's how you set each of the charging options (plus "no charge", of course):

If you're using the Bango Relay Service (see Chapter 9), which uses a single Bango Number to charge for multiple items of content, you're limited to using one charging option for all those items covered by that Bango Number.

Note that with Bango Relay functionality you can vary the amount charged for each item of content dynamically (you set the charges in your own code rather than the Bango system). If you don't use this functionality the price is fixed for each Bango Number.

## Currency issues

When you buy a Bango package you nomimate a trading currency. This currency is used between you and Bango—for paying Bango's fees and for receiving your proportion of your site's revenue—and also for setting charges for each Bango Number you own in that package. (If you have multiple packages you can nominate a different trading currency for each if you want.) Your trading currency should typically be the same currency your bank account uses.

The trading currency is not necessarily the same as the currency your customers are charged in. Your customers can choose to be charged in pounds sterling, euros or US dollars, whatever your trading currency. Bango transparently converts prices to the customer's chosen currency so you don't have to worry about it. For ease of administration Bango updates its currency exchange rates at the start of each month. Depending on the overall fluctuation in exchange rates, this means you may receive less (or more) revenue than you expect over that month.

# Chapter 19
# Tracking site usage

How popular is your site? Is it getting more popular or less popular? How can you measure the effectiveness of your promotional activities?

Of course, your monthly earnings are a strong indicator of how your site's doing. But this is a crude—though welcome!—measure. Fortunately the Bango Members' Lounge web site lets you view much more detailed statistics on all of your Bango Numbers, slicing and dicing the data every which way. In this chapter we'll describe how you can interpret the data into the information you need to help grow your business.

## What's available in the Members' Lounge?

Each time anyone accesses a Bango Number, the Bango system logs the time and date and the amount spent (if any). Within the Manage Content section of the Members' Lounge, you choose Usage Info to access all the hit data for the Bango Numbers in your package. The data is never more than 10 minutes old—so you're seeing near-real-time statistics.

By default the Usage Info page shows you a summary for the current month. This shows, for each day in the month, the total number of accesses to the Bango Numbers in your package, the number of paid-for accesses, and the total value of those paid-for accesses. The data is displayed both as a list and as a graph.

Now you can:

- Display the summary for a different month, by choosing the month from the drop-down list.
- Display hour-by-hour data for one day within the month, by choosing the day from the calendar or from the list.

- Display the data by Bango Number rather than by date by clicking View by Number.

- Change which of your Bango Numbers are included in the report, using the top-right section of the page. Select a Bango Number from the Included Numbers list and click < to exclude that Bango Number from the report. You can use the << and >> buttons to quickly exclude or include all Bango Numbers in the report.

- Download a Microsoft Excel spreadsheet file for the month you're currently viewing. This includes hour-by-hour data for every day in the month and every Bango Number in your package.

Bango may add more features to the Usage Info page over time.

# Turning data into information

Raw data is like compost: indispensable, but a means to an end rather than an end in itself. The raw data available on the Usage Info page is incredibly useful, but becomes even more useful when processed. Turning data into information helps you make meaningful judgements about the data—to learn from it, and to grow your business from the results.

Bango doesn't try to interpret your data for you: it provides you with the compost, and lets you decide where to sprinkle it. A simple but effective tactic is to compare different portions of the data. Let's look at some progressively more useful ways to do this.

## Trends over time

The easiest way to analyse your data is to look for simple trends over time. Here are a few things you can do:

- **Compare a sequence of months.** Can you spot any patterns in the totals for each month? You might find that you have a steady growth, even if the totals for each day are sometimes up and sometimes down.

- **Look at moving averages.** Take the average total for January, February and March, and compare it to the average total for February, March and April. Keep going, *sliding* the three months along. This tends to smooth out outstandingly bad or good months and give you a better idea of longer-term trends.

- **Try to find yearly patterns.** Many businesses experience a downturn during August as people go on holiday, and a big boost in the run-up to Christmas. When comparing one month against another, it helps to know whether the months are typically good or bad earners.

- **Try to find monthly, weekly or even daily patterns.** For example, your earnings might typically be lower in the third week of the month as people wait for their monthly salary to be paid. Or you might discover that Monday is your best day of the week as that's the day after the weekly singles charts are published. There are obvious daily patterns—not many people buy content during the middle of the night—but see if you can spot less obvious ones. Do you get a boost during the lunch hour at work? If you're selling globally, can you tell which market is most lucrative by looking at peaks and figuring out time differences between countries?

- **Compare the performance of individual Bango Numbers.** With data available for each Bango Number, you can look at patterns and averages for any combinations of your Bango Numbers. For example, if you sell both games and ringtones in your mobile shop you might find they sell at different times of day, or different days of the week.

- **Compare "before" and "after" periods.** If you change your site in a significant way—add lots of new content, introduce special offers, redesign the way that customers purchase content, and so on—then look at the data before and after the change. If the numbers go up (taking into account patterns and trends), the site change was a good thing. If the numbers go down, then you've made a mistake. Rethink your changes.

## Campaign comparison

Is a promotional campaign working as effectively as it could? Would a different campaign be better or worse? One way to find out is to run both in parallel, using different Bango Numbers. You can then analyse the statistics for each Bango Number to see which campaign is more effective.

It's a good idea to run these comparisons in parallel to avoid any date-based patterns and trends overwhelming the true data. For example, campaign X in July might appear to be more effective than campaign Y in August simply because more people are on holiday in August and so don't see the campaign.

You might discover that one campaign is significantly better than the other simply by looking at the raw data: perhaps campaign X receives ten times as many hits as campaign Y in total. More likely you'll want to "drill down" the data and see how the campaigns compare over specific time periods. You might discover that each campaign has its strengths, and you can use that information to produce a new campaign Z that beats both the others.

## Conversion ratio

A conversion ratio tells you how many of your browsers buy. Put simply, if you have 100 visitors and 15 purchases, your conversion ratio is 15/100 or 15%. No matter how many visitors you receive, a conversion ratio gives a good indication of the effectiveness of your site.

One goal of your mobile shop should be to maximise your conversion ratios. This is a slightly different goal than simply maximising the number of visitors to your site: doubling the number of browsers might double the number of buyers, but it doesn't necessarily make your site any more effective at convincing people to buy. And remember: you have as many conversion ratios as you have items to sell.

The raw data available from the Members' Lounge includes both the total number of visits and the total number of paid-for visits, for each Bango Number, for every hour of every day. You can use this data to track conversion ratios over time. Here's an example chart that shows how a site's conversion ratio for a special offer changed over three months:

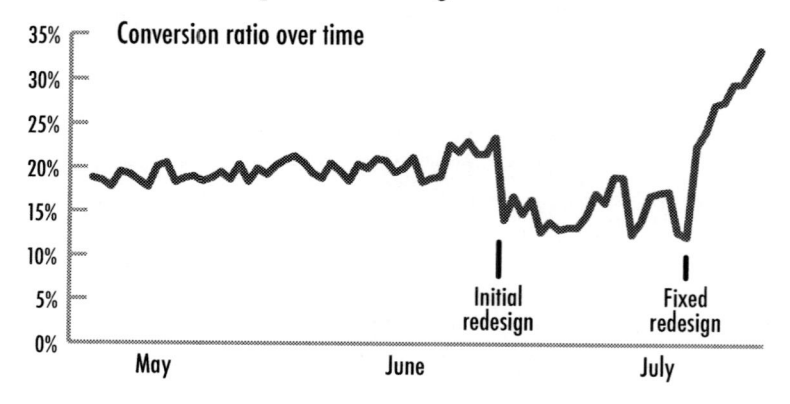

**Conversion ratio over time**

(Chart showing conversion ratio from May through July, ranging 0%–35%. Ratio hovers around 20% in May and early June, drops after "Initial redesign" in mid-June to around 10–15%, then rises sharply after "Fixed redesign" in July to over 30%.)

Part III — Attracting customers to your site—and keeping them

The chart shows a slowly growing conversion ratio, followed by a dramatic drop in mid-June. The cause was a site redesign—in this case, one that inadvertently made it less likely for browsers to take up the special offer than before. Once this was noticed and fixed, conversion rates for the offer improved significantly.

## Categorising customers

Throughout the book we've emphasised how important it is to know your customers. If you don't know your customers, changes you make to your mobile shop will be less effective than they could be—even damaging to your business. The statistics available on the Usage Info page give you an excellent way to help determine whether you're on the right track.

Bango has several years' experience in analysing patterns of customer behaviour. With millions of mobile content buyers, thousands of content providers and dozens of content categories, Bango is extremely well-placed to understand what makes customers tick.

From its data Bango has identified three distinct types of mobile content consumer: classified as *Grazers*, *Porkers* and *Nibblers*.

- **Grazers** consume at a small but steady rate, month after month. They're the most common inhabitants of the mobile "savannah", consistently spending between £5 and £20 each month, and rarely busting their budget.

- **Porkers** are about twenty times less common than Grazers, but spend between £30-£50 per month and are happy to go over-budget on occasion. Some spend over £100 a month on average, and £300-£400 in peak months. Porkers use Bango's "Favourites" facility and the Bango Directory, and are keen foragers for new content.

- **Nibblers** consume small amounts, and only rarely do they purchase anything at all. They're more interested in niche markets than more mass-market content such as ringtones or images.

What can we learn from these observations?

- Keep Grazers happy by feeding them with new content regularly. Grazers are predictable, reliable customers.

- Target Porkers by enticing them with special offers and subscriptions to satisfy their feeding frenzies. Include clear "buy more" links on download pages to keep them moving across the savannah to more content.

Bango has also identified other interesting buying behaviour:

- **Binging.** Occasionally, Nibblers and Grazers spend between five and ten times their normal monthly amount all at once. In effect, they take on the role of a Porker for a day. Sometimes a hangover follows a binge, with a lower-than-normal spend for a few months.
- **Classic Bill Shock.** Here a consumer with Porker-like behaviour turns into a Grazer or a Nibbler after receiving the monthly bill. This might occur as a customer upgrades to a new GPRS colour phone and goes on a personalisation spree.
- **Passing Fad.** Some consumers shift from one content type to another, for example moving from ringtones to games, as they get bored. The amount spent remains steady, however.

You can use these categories to help understand the statistics for your own site. Think about how you might turn Nibblers into Grazers, and how you can encourage Porkers to feed.

Chapter 20
# Doing business with Bango

In this final chapter we'll explain the process of doing business with Bango: how you pay your fees for use of the Bango Service, and how Bango pays you your earnings—the slice of the revenue earned by your site. There's also a short section on VAT—which you'll need to understand if your site becomes popular and lucrative enough.

## Paying for Bango packages

You pay monthly to subscribe to the Bango Service. For the first month you pay by credit/debit card (Pro, Focus and Express customers can alternatively pay by bank transfer). If you are a Micro customer Bango will deduct your subscription fee from your credit/debit card each month. If you are a Pro, Focus or Express customer, how you pay in subsequent months depends on how much you earned in the previous month.

- If your earnings are greater than your subscription payment then Bango simply deducts the appropriate amount from your earnings.
- If you haven't earned enough that month Bango will use the credit/debit card information you supplied for the first month to extract payment from you. If you didn't use a credit or debit card then Bango will contact you by email or surface mail to arrange payment.

Your subscription payment is due each month on the same day—the day of the month on which you originally signed up.

If Bango can't automatically obtain payment and you haven't paid your subscription within 14 days of the due date, Bango will suspend your account. If there's still no payment after another 14 days the account will be closed and your Bango Numbers released.

# Your earnings

You receive 60% of the revenue earned by your site. Around 35% is taken by the mobile operator or billing provider and Bango takes roughly 5% as a service charge. For example, if you charge £2 for a ringtone then you earn £1.20 commission (VAT will be deducted from this amount) each time someone buys that ringtone. The 60% rate is the same whether you charge 1p or £10 for your content.

Your earnings accumulate in the Bango system. You can use the Money Earned page of the Bango Member's Lounge whenever you like to check how much you're earning. On the first day of the following month you can see the total amount. If that amount is above a certain threshold then your earnings are payable; if not, then the earnings are carried forward to the next month. This threshold helps keep Bango's administration down—and keeps your fees down too. Currently the payment threshold is £50, €50 or $50, depending on the currency you chose as your trading currency when you signed up to the Bango Service.

If your earnings exceed the threshold, there's only one small hurdle of financial regulations to jump before the money appears in your bank account. Before Bango can pay you, it must produce a *purchase order* and you must issue an *invoice* in return. If you're unfamiliar with these standard business forms then don't worry: the Bango system helps you out.

In brief, a purchase order is issued to a supplier as an official request for a product or service. Purchase orders state what's being requested and the agreed price. An invoice is issued by a supplier as an official request for payment, and is often supplied with the product in response to a purchase order. Invoices explain exactly what payment is required for, and how much is required.

Financial departments use purchase orders and invoices to keep track of their incoming and outgoing payments and run their budget more effectively. Tax officials may examine purchase orders and invoices to check that the appropriate amount of tax has been paid.

Even if you're selling content through Bango as an individual rather than a business, you still need to deal with purchase orders and invoices.

On the first of each month, if your earnings exceed the threshold, the Money Earned page for a package in the Member's Lounge will help you print out a purchase order. This is a purchase order *from* Bango *to* you, effectively authorising the "purchase" of your earnings.

In return you must issue an invoice before Bango can pay you. There's a sample invoice on the Money Earned page of the Member's Lounge to help you include all the information Bango needs to process the payment efficiently.

Here's an example of how you collect your money from Bango. Let's assume you sold a lot of content in January.

On February 1st the Money Earned page shows a purchase order for January's content, for the value of the money Bango is paying to you. You need to send Bango an invoice for that amount (using the sample invoice if necessary to help include everything you need).

As long as you send both purchase order and invoice to Bango by March 15th, Bango will pay you by the end of March.

# Paying package fees using your earnings

If you're a Pro, Focus or Express customer, you have an extra benefit: if your earnings for a month exceed the subscription cost of your Bango package then Bango will deduct the subscription payment from your earnings when paying an invoice. Two examples will show how this works in practice.

## When earnings are greater than package fees

Robby has bought a package for £100 a month (amount chosen to make the maths easier: check with Bango for actual prices).

- Robby earns £150 in April from content sales and invoices Bango for £150 on May 1st.
- Robby's package renews on May 12th.
- On May 12th, Bango looks back to April and sees that Robby's earnings are greater than the package fee. Bango invoices Robby for £100.
- When Bango makes the payment to Robby, they pay him £50 (£150 earnings minus £100 package fee).

### When earnings are less than package fees

Colin has also bought a £100-per-month package.

- Colin earns £80 in April and invoices Bango for £80 on May 1st.
- Colin's package renews on May 24th.
- On May 24th, Bango looks back to April and sees that Colin's earnings are less than the package fee. Bango invoices Colin for £100.
- Full payment for the package (£100) is taken from Colin's credit card.
- When Bango makes the payment to Colin they pay him £80.

## VAT

We recommend you contact a qualified accountant for financial advice on tax matters. Here's a summary to help you understand how to proceed.

VAT, or Value-Added Tax, is a tax charged by suppliers on the goods or services they supply. Not all suppliers are allowed to charge VAT: a UK supplier must be registered for VAT with HM Customs and Excise to do so (other countries have similar schemes: contact your local tax authorities for details). Suppliers without a VAT registration must not charge VAT.

There are rules governing when a supplier must register for VAT. Generally it depends on how much you have earned or expect to earn within a time period. If a supplier's (anticipated) earnings exceed the threshold set by the rules then it must register. Beneath that threshold registration is voluntary.

There are also rules governing when a VAT-registered supplier is allowed to charge VAT. For example, it depends on the country the supplier's customer lives in.

Bango is VAT-registered and will add VAT to package subscriptions and other prices where appropriate. Bango handles VAT payments from your end users within the European Union. If your content is exported outside the EU, Bango also handles taxation requirements. (If you export a great deal of content, contact Bango as you may be able to recover extra revenues.)

As a revenue-earning content provider you are also considered a supplier for VAT purposes. If not already VAT-registered you need to decide whether to apply for registration based on the current rules. If you are registered then the invoices you send to Bango must charge VAT on your earnings.

Part IV
# Appendixes

*Appendix 1*
# Device information

There are a bewildering number of phones on the market today. Phone functionality is improving all the time: new features appear regularly, screen sizes are increasing and ringtones are becoming more sophisticated. This makes targeting the entire market seemingly impossible: there's too much variety. How can you determine whether your content will work with any particular phone?

It would be foolish to try to describe the capabilities of each phone here—the information would immediately be out of date and take up most of the book. But we can help you find out the information you need to answer many of the trickier problems.

There are two primary sources we recommend for device information: the WURFL and UAProf. They might sound like characters from a 1950s B-movie but before long you'll be treating them as close friends.

## The WURFL

The *WURFL*—the Wireless Universal Resource File—was created and is maintained by three people: Laszlo Nadai, Luca Passani and Andrea Trasatti. These three, who call themselves the Holy Trinity, realised the need for a central repository for device information and made it happen, with help from many other contributors worldwide.

The WURFL is a single XML file (available from http://wurfl.sourceforge.net) that describes the abilities and constraints of every mobile phone (and other wireless devices) the Holy Trinity and their contributors have been able to get their hands on. It's an open source project, and you're free to take the WURFL and use it in any way you wish—as long as you make public any changes to the file (preferably by sending those changes back to the maintainers).

At the time of writing, the WURFL is 380 KB—pretty large, and daunting at first glance, but packed with information. It's worth investing the time to understand how to extract the information you need.

## Example

The WURFL file has a section for each device. Since many devices are similar to one another—phones from the same manufacturer often have similar features—the file uses *fallback* values to avoid repeating the same information for each device. These fallback values can themselves fall back, all the way to a hypothetical "generic" device that defines the capabilities shared by every device in the file (unless overridden). This makes the process of discovering a particular phone's complete set of capabilities a game of follow-the-fallback. Let's look at an example: the Nokia 6610.

```
<device user_agent="Nokia6610"
        fall_back="nokia_generic_series40"
        id="nokia_6610_ver1">
 <group id="product_info">
  <capability name="model_name" value="6610"/>
 </group>
 <group id="sound_format">
  <capability name="midi_monophonic" value="true"/>
  <capability name="midi_polyphonic" value="true"/>
  <capability name="sp_midi" value="true"/>
  <capability name="nokia_ringtone" value="true"/>
  <capability name="voices" value="4"/>
 </group>
</device>
<device user_agent="Nokia6610/1.0"
        fall_back="nokia_6610_ver1"
        id="nokia_6610_ver1_sub00"/>
<device user_agent="Nokia6610/1.0 (3.09) Profile/MIDP-1.0 Configuration/CLDC-1.0"
        fall_back="nokia_6610_ver1"
        id="nokia_6610_ver1_sub309"/>
<device user_agent="Nokia6610/1.0 (4.18) Profile/MIDP-1.0 Configuration/CLDC-1.0"
        fall_back="nokia_6610_ver1"
        id="nokia_6610_ver1_sub418"/>
<device user_agent="Nokia6610/1.0 (4.28) Profile/MIDP-1.0 Configuration/CLDC-1.0"
        fall_back="nokia_6610_ver1"
        id="nokia_6610_ver1_sub428"/>
```

WURFL interpretation starts with the device's *user agent* string. This is unique to each device model and version, and sent along with every request to a web server. You look within each `device` element in the WURFL file for the `user_agent` attribute value that's the longest match for your device's user agent—and that's your starting point.

In the example above there are five `device` elements, each referring to slightly different user agents. Let's say our phone's user agent includes `Nokia6610/1.0 (4.18) Profile/MIDP-1.0 Configuration/CLDC-1.0`. That means we match the fourth `device` element above, so our ID (our unique identifier within the WURFL file) is `nokia_6610_ver1_sub418` and our fallback for all settings not defined within our own `device` element is the device with ID `nokia_6610_ver1`.

Here our matching `device` element is empty—none of the capabilities is different from the fallback. In this case the WURFL maintainers are using this entry simply to record the existence of a new version of this phone and to confirm that its functionality hasn't changed. (You'll notice three other similar empty devices.)

To find out our phone's functionality, then, we must look at the `device` element matching our fallback ID. That's the first `device` element in our example above. Within that fallback element we see some `group` and `capability` elements that should make sense. For example, within the `sound_format` group we see that the Nokia 6610 can accept both monophonic and polyphonic MIDI files. (Look on the WURFL site for a description of every capability.)

Not everything is defined by our fallback device: notice that there's *another* fallback to follow, in this case to the device with ID `nokia_generic_series40` (not included in our example above, but defined in the full WURFL file). If you follow the fallbacks yourself you'll find this falls back further to a Nokia series 30 device, then series 20, then a hypothetical "Nokia generic" device, and then to the granddaddy of them all, `generic` itself.

Within `generic` you'd see the `midi_polyphonic` capability defined as `false`. That's why it was redefined as `true` by our first fallback device above: to override all the other fallbacks.

# UAProf

In contrast to the WURFL, *UAProf* (User Agent Profile) was created by the WAP Forum (now known as the Open Mobile Alliance)—the coalition of vendors developing the WAP standard. (UAProf is itself based on the Composite Capabilities/Preferences Profile (CC/PP) specification of the World Wide Web Consortium, the body that effectively sets standards for the web.)

With UAProf the capabilities of each mobile device are stored in an file available on the internet. Each UAProf-compatible device knows where its UAProf file is, and whenever it sends a request to a web server (either directly or through a WAP gateway) it includes the URL of its UAProf file (in an HTTP header "Profile"). The web server can if necessary retrieve the file and extract the information it needs to customise the content for the phone. Unlike the WURFL, a UAProf file is the copyright of the phone manufacturer.

There's a good overview of UAProf on Nokia's web site. Go to http://www.forum.nokia.com/documents and search for UAProf.

## Example

UAProf files use RDF to describe capabilities (RDF is an XML application, just to add more acronyms to the mix). If you don't understand RDF it'll look slightly scary at first, but seeing a few UAProf files should help make things clear.

A good source of UAProf files is http://w3development.de/rdf/uaprof_repository/. But note that phones themselves don't point to these profiles: they instead point to URLs on the manufacturer web site.

A UAProf file has several sections describing, for example, the phone's hardware, software, network characteristics, browser capabilities, WAP characteristics, push characteristics and MMS characteristics. Each section is stored within an `rdf:Description` element within the file, which is itself stored within a `prf:component` element. Here's an example from the BrowserUA—browser user agent capabilities—section of the Sony Ericsson P900's file:

```
    <prf:component>
      <rdf:Description rdf:ID="BrowserUA">
      <rdf:type rdf:resource="http://www.wapforum.org/profiles/
UAPROF/ccppschema-20010330#BrowserUA"/>
         <prf:BrowserName>Sony Ericsson</prf:BrowserName>
         <prf:FramesCapable>No</prf:FramesCapable>
         <prf:TablesCapable>Yes</prf:TablesCapable>
      </rdf:Description>
    </prf:component>
```

You can see here that the `prf:TablesCapable` element specifies that the browser on this phone understands how to display tables. If you want to know what each element within a section means, look at the URL defined in the rdf:resource attribute and then search for that section (here, look at the www.wapforum.org URL and search for BrowserUA).

## Which to use?

Both the WURFL and UAProf are useful sources of information. At first glance you might think you could choose one of them and ignore the other. It's true that much of the information they store overlaps. But both are useful:

- The WURFL contains some information about bugs and quirks. For example, one capability is named `break_list_of_links_with_br_element_recommended`.

- UAProf is more specific about things like supported file formats: it lists them using standard MIME types, such as `video/3gpp` and `audio/mp3`. These files are also the manufacturers' own information so in theory they're more reliable.

You can check the Bango Member's Lounge web site each month for details of the most popular devices. The graphic on the next page shows the top twenty handsets for March 2005.

| Position | | Handset | Percentage |
|---|---|---|---|
| 1 | — | Nokia 6230 | 20.30% |
| 2 | ▲ | Sony Ericsson K700 | 8.22% |
| 3 | ▲ | Nokia 3100 | 7.34% |
| 4 | ▼ | Nokia 6610i | 6.16% |
| 5 | NEW | Nokia 3220 | 5.46% |
| 6 | NEW | Sony Ericsson K500 | 5.13% |
| 7 | ▼ | Nokia 7250i | 4.67% |
| 8 | ▼ | Sony Ericsson T610 | 4.64% |
| 9 | NEW | Samsung D500 | 4.50% |
| 10 | ▼ | Nokia 3510i | 4.17% |
| 11 | NEW | Sony Ericsson T230 | 3.43% |
| 12 | ▼ | Samsung E700 | 3.41% |
| 13 | ▲ | Nokia 6600 | 3.22% |
| 14 | ▼ | Nokia 3200 | 3.10% |
| 15 | ▼ | Sony Ericsson T630 | 3.04% |
| 16 | ▲ | Nokia 7610 | 2.93% |
| 17 | ▼ | Samsung E800 | 2.70% |
| 18 | ▼ | Nokia 3200 | 2.63% |
| 19 | ▼ | Nokia 7600 | 2.50% |
| 20 | ▼ | Motorola V220 | 2.45% |

Appendix 2
# Web server issues

This appendix covers two important web server configuration issues: ensuring that web servers process `index.wml` files correctly, and that they assign the appropriate MIME types to WML-related files.

## Directory index files

When a user goes to a "directory" URL—a URL that doesn't specify a file at the end, for example `http://bango.com/products/`—the web server must decide what to do. It typically does one of three things:

- It displays a directory listing—a list of all files in that directory. Sometimes this is what you want, but not usually.

- It displays a "directory listing denied" message. You'll generally do this when you don't want casual surfers to find out what files are in the directory.

- It chooses an index file from those in that directory, based on rules set in its configuration, and displays that instead. This is often what you want—it means you can use shorter URLs in your site and in your promotional material.

Most often a web server is configured to pick an index file from a list of possibilities, often files called `index.html`, `index.htm`, `index.php` and so on. (The prefix `index` is just a convention: you can use any name you want.) If you're adding WML files to your own web server you should consider adding `index.wml` to the list to ensure you can use directory URLs successfully. Web servers aren't normally configured by default to do this.

### Configuring your web server's directory indexing

Your web server's documentation should include information on how to configure directory index files.

For Apache web servers, you can do any of the following:

- Edit the web server's configuration file, usually `httpd.conf`, and add or edit an existing `DirectoryIndex` directive to include `index.wml`. You'll need to restart the web server for the change to take effect.

- If `.htaccess` files are enabled for a directory, you can add the `DirectoryIndex` directive to any appropriate `.htaccess` file to set the directory index configuration within that directory and its subdirectories. Changes to `.htaccess` files take effect immediately.

For Microsoft IIS web servers, use the Microsoft Management Console.

## WML-related MIME types

A web server may need to be configured to associate the proper MIME type with a file. MIME types are detected by browsers (both mobile internet browsers on a phone and fixed internet browsers on a PC or Mac) and help the browsers to take the most appropriate action with the file. For example, GIF image files have the MIME type `image/gif`: the browser then knows to display the image on-screen rather than, for example, try and play the file as a ringtone.

MIME types are allocated by a central authority, the Internet Assigned Numbers Authority. All currently allocated MIME types are listed at `http://www.iana.org/assignments/media-types/`.

Most MIME types are already properly configured for a web server. However, some WML MIME types may not be configured. The usual symptom of this is the source of a WML file being displayed, complete with < and > symbols.

The WML-related MIME types are:

| MIME type | File extension | Description |
|---|---|---|
| text/vnd.wap.wml | wml | WML source file |
| application/vnd.wap.wmlc | wmlc | Compiled WML files |
| text/vnd.wap.wmlscript | wmls | WMLScript source files |
| application/vnd.wap.wmlscriptc | wmlsc | Compiled WMLScript files |
| image/vnd.wap.wbmp | wbmp | Wireless Bitmap files |

## Configuring your web server's MIME types

Your web server's documentation should include information on how to configure MIME types.

For Apache web servers, you can do any of the following:

- Add the appropriate lines to the web server's mime.types file. You'll find this file in the configuration directory for the web server. Follow the same pattern as the other lines in the file. You'll need to restart the web server for the change to take effect.

- Add lines of the form `AddType text/vnd.wap.wml wml` to the web server's configuration file, usually `httpd.conf`. You'll need to restart the web server for the change to take effect.

- If `.htaccess` files are enabled for a directory, you can add lines of the form `AddType text/vnd.wap.wml wml` to any appropriate `.htaccess` file to ensure the correct MIME types are set for files served from that directory and its subdirectories. Changes to `.htaccess` files take effect immediately.

For Microsoft IIS web servers, use the Microsoft Management Console.

*Appendix 3*
# Bango Txt Trigger guidelines and requirements

The Bango Txt Trigger Service (described in Chapter 15) is paid for by the user. In the UK, the Independent Committee for the Supervision of Standards of Telephone Information (ICSTIS, http://www.icstis.org.uk) sets down guidelines and requirements for content providers to follow to ensure users get exactly what they expect.

## ICSTIS code of practice

ICSTIS sets out a code of practice that must be followed if you are charging for information or services over a telephony network.

The main points that must be adhered to when promoting the Bango Txt Trigger are:

- You must clearly indicate the maximum price the user will be charged (in this case, £1.50 for the text message) in any promotion or advertising.
- Your identity and contact details must be clearly stated in any promotion. The identity means the name of the company, partnership or sole trader. The contact details must consist of either the full postal address (including postcode), a PO Box number (including postcode) or a telephone helpline number (charged at no more than UK national rate). (A PO Box may not be used in the case of employment, employment information and business opportunity services.)

We recommend that you contact ICSTIS if you're in any doubt about your obligations.

## Appendix 4
# Payment for your content

The Bango system automatically presents your users with payment options. The system determines the best payment option for the user and presents this as the default (the user can choose another).

The default option is chosen based on the country the user is in, the network operator they're using and the amount of money you want them to spend.

## Premium reverse SMS

In some countries, for example the UK, Bango sends your users a special *Premium* SMS message to collect money from them, paid on their bill or by reducing their pre-paid credit. The user experience differs for operator-verified users and unverified users.

### Operator-verified users

Through special agreements with mobile operators, Bango is able to determine a user's phone number at the time they try to purchase content. They're then presented with the option to pay "on my bill (txt)".

Selecting this option causes the Bango system to send the customer a *reverse SMS*: a text message that the customer pays to *receive*. The cost of the message will be the smallest multiple of a fixed amount (£1.50 in the UK) that covers the cost of the content they want to purchase. For example, if they want to buy a £2.50 ringtone they will receive a text message that costs them £3.00. Any money left over, here 50p, is credited to the customer's Bango account and available to spend on future transactions.

Once payment has been collected, the customer is redirected to the content they've purchased.

### Unverified users

If a customer tries to access Bango-enabled content that has a charge set against it, and the Bango system can't detect their phone number directly, they're prompted to send a standard SMS text message such as "go payment" (or "go" plus the phone-spelling word form of a valid Bango Number) to a Bango short code (see the Members' Lounge for the current list of short codes).

When the Bango system receives the message it creates a Bango user identity for the customer and the user is now verified. The customer can then return to your site and start spending.

(The Bango Txt Trigger Service lets you optimise this process: you advertise the "go" method of accessing your site using the word form of your Bango Number, which will identify the user, prepay for content, and redirect straight to your site. For more on the Bango Txt Trigger Service see Chapter 15.)

### Operator billing systems

Bango has strategic relationships with key mobile operators worldwide. These relationships allow Bango to integrate with the operators' own billing systems to make payment easier. Check the Bango Members' Lounge for the current list of operator billing relationships.

When the Bango system detects that a customer can be charged using an operator billing system, it presents the option "pay on my bill" when the customer tries to purchase content. The precise amount charged to the customer's bill may be greater than the price of the content, as some operators may impose minimum transaction costs.

### Debit/credit cards

Bango allows customers to pay for your content using their debit card or credit card. This option is invaluable for customers unable or unwilling to purchase content using premium reverse SMS or operator billing systems, and extends your marketplace to millions of potential customers wordwide.

When a customer chooses this payment option they're asked to supply their debit/credit card number, expiry date and three-digit security code as with any other debit/credit card transaction.

Once payment is authorised the Bango system presents the customer with a receipt number and their personal "fingerprint" number (their unique Bango ID). The customer can later visit http://bango.net/receipt from a PC or Mac web browser and type in the receipt number and their fingerprint to obtain a printable receipt.

# PIN codes

Customers in certain countries can purchase 8-digit PIN codes by ringing a premium-rate IVR (Interactive Voice Response) number. These PIN codes can then be used to pay for content. For example:

- In the UK, customers ring 0907 787 9904. The call lasts approximately two minutes and costs £3.00 in total.
- In Germany, customers ring 0190 840 562. The call lasts approximately two minutes and costs €3.72 in total.

In each case the PIN code is given at the end of the call.

When a customer wants to purchase content they can select to pay "by PIN code". If the cost of the content is less than £3.00 (or €3.72, as appropriate) the difference is credited to the customer's Bango account to spend on other Bango-enabled content.

Bango can supply you with PIN codes at a discount from "face value" if you want to sell them through your own channels.